Getting Parents Involved in Their Children's Education

By
Larry E. Decker,
Gloria A. Gregg, and
Virginia A. Decker

American Association of School Administrators

Contents

Preface III

Introduction V
Today's Families and Communities
Schools Need Help
The Local Challenge
The National Challenge

Chapter 1: The Rationale for Parent and Community Involvement 1
Changing Attitudes
What the Research Says
Do Parents Want To Be Involved?
What Keeps Some Parents from Being Involved?
Who Should Take the Lead?
What Practices Encourage Involvement?

Chapter 2: Assessing School-Family Relations 11
A Sampling of Surveys and Questionnaires

Chapter 3: A Framework for Parent Involvement 21
Four Models of Parent Involvement
Theory to Practice
Types of Parent Involvement
A Sampling of Involvement Designs

Chapter 4: Principles and Strategies for Implementation 47
What Do Successful Programs Have in Common?
Implementation Strategies
Setting the Tone Through Leadership
Inservice Training
Dealing with Pressure Groups

Chapter 5: Policy Statements: Making It Official 67
Enlisting Board Support
School District Policies
Administrative Considerations

Chapter 6: Involving Hard-To-Reach and At-Risk Parents 73
New Directions in Parent Involvement
Success with Urban Families
Keeping Parents of Older Students Involved

Conclusion 82

Bibliography 84

Resources 90

PREFACE

When it comes to making sure students get a good education, schools simply can't do it alone. Education, at its best, is a team effort involving schools, the communities they serve, students, and parents.

We hope this timely book focusing on parent involvement will help school systems better understand the attitudes that foster or inhibit involvement.

Authors Larry Decker, Gloria Gregg, and Virginia Decker take a look at effective frameworks for parent involvement. They also pinpoint a number of effective programs that could serve as springboards for the type of involvement that will ultimately lead to an even better education for students in the classroom. Finally, they suggest board policies that are the very foundation for parent involvement efforts.

Historically, AASA has supported appropriate and effective involvement of parents in the schools. However, during the 1980s and 1990s, our surveys have shown an overwhelming demand for even better ways to get parents on the education team. That's why we've published this book, which joins a distinguished family of publications devoted to this topic that is so important to education.

Paul D. Houston
Executive Director
American Association of School Administrators

Many schools are like islands set apart from the mainland of life by a deep moat of convention and tradition. A drawbridge is lowered at certain periods during the day in order that the part-time inhabitants may cross over to the island in the morning and back to the mainland at night.

Why do these young people go out to the island? To learn how to live on the mainland. When they reach the island, they are provided with books that tell about life on the mainland. Once in a while, as a special treat, the bus takes a few of the more favored islanders on a tour of the mainland. But this is allowed only when reading books about the mainland has been completed.

After the last inhabitant of the island has left in the afternoon, the drawbridge is raised. Janitors clean up the island, and the lights go out. No one is left except perhaps a lonely watchman keeping a vigil along the shoreline. The island is lifeless most of Saturday and Sunday. The drawbridge collects cobwebs all summer and during other long holidays.

One evening a year, the island's lights burn late for an event called graduation. Then the islanders depart, never to set foot on the island again.

After the graduates leave the island for the last time, they are bombarded by problems of life on the mainland. Sometimes one of the graduates may mutter, "On the island I read something about that in a book."

— William G. Carr, former executive secretary,
  National Education Association,
  speaking to the 1942 National Congress
  of Parents and Teachers

INTRODUCTION

More than 50 years ago, William G. Carr, then executive secretary of the National Education Association, described the typical public school as an island connected to the mainland by a drawbridge. Monday through Friday, the bridge was let down every morning and afternoon for children to come and go, and one or two evenings a year for adults from the mainland to visit on brief, ceremonial occasions. Ironically, Carr pointed out, the main purpose of the island stronghold was to teach the children how to live on the mainland.

Although Carr's island image persists with some validity, today's educators are making efforts every day to connect schools with students' homes and communities. However, these attempts will be successful only if schools accurately assess the realities of family and community life and design substantive ways to involve parents and community members in their children's education.

TODAY'S FAMILIES AND COMMUNITIES

When reaching out to parents, schools can no longer fall back on past practices based on an outdated mold of the family. In fact, one could argue that families don't fit any mold any more. The American family has changed dramatically over the last several decades. In 1955, 60 percent of American households had what appeared to be, at least on the outside, a "Leave It to Beaver" family: working father, housewife mother, and two children. By 1980, the percentage had dropped to 11 percent, and by 1992, to 6 percent, according to author and futurist Harold Hodgkinson.

In 1993, Hodgkinson used 1990 census data to make the following observations about the current status of children and families:

- Eighty-two percent of all children under 18 have working mothers.
- Six of 10 mothers of preschool children (under age 6) work outside the home on at least a part-time basis.
- Thirteen percent of all children are regularly hungry.
- Approximately 350,000 children are born annually to drug-addicted mothers.
- Of every 100,000 juveniles, 166 are behind bars.
- Of households headed by a single woman with children under 18, 75 percent are in poverty; the median income is $10,982.
- In 1988, 57 percent of families and individuals could not qualify for a loan to buy a median-priced home in their community.

These statistics are not used here to point a finger at women in any way. What they do show is that more and more, children are being raised by one person instead of two, and they are facing social and economic problems within their homes that would be daunting to the strongest person.

The *1993 Kids Count Data Book*, published by the Annie E. Casey Foundation and the Center for the Study of Social Policy, presents more sobering statistics based on the 1990 census:

- Single teens give birth to 8.7 percent of all babies born in the United States.
- Out of every 100,000 youths age 10-17, 466 are arrested for a violent crime. For 18-year-olds, the rate increases to 1,348 of every 100,000.
- At least 19.8 percent of children under 18 live in poverty; the percentage is 23.6 for children under 6.
- Almost 25 percent of children live in single-parent families.
- More than 6 million children age 5-7 do not speak English at home.

Families at risk

Kids Count calculates a "vulnerable family index" based on three risk factors: a mother under 20 when the first child was born, a mother who had not completed high school when the first child was born, and unmarried parents. Of the roughly 1.7 million families formed with the birth of a first baby in 1990, 11 percent had all three risk factors; 24 percent had two risk factors; and 45 percent had one risk factor.

More Kids At Risk

Applying the *Kids Count* risk factors to children ages 7-12 in 1988, who lived in poverty and who were in the lower half of their classes academically, the following was found:

Children in Poverty
All three risk factors	79%
Two risk factors	48%
One risk factor	26%
No risk factors	8%

Children in Lower Half of Class Academically
All three risk factors	58%
Two risk factors	53%
One risk factor	47%
No risk factors	30%

The Children's Defense Fund, a children's advocacy group, reported more grim news in 1991:
- In 1988, 450,700 children were described as runaways and another 127,100 as throwaways (told to leave home or not sought after they ran away).
- Among students who entered ninth grade in 1984, approximately 29 percent did not graduate from high school in 1988. The 1988 graduation rate for 18- to

19-year-old white students was 74 percent; for African American students, 58.4 percent; and for Latino students, 52.3 percent.
- Homicide is the second leading cause of death among all adolescents and young adults.
- In 1989, 2.4 million children were reported to be abused or neglected, a 10 percent increase over the number in 1988.

Seconds Count in America

Every 35 seconds an infant is born into poverty.
Every 2 minutes an infant is born to a mother who received late or no prenatal care.
Every 2 minutes an infant is born at low birthweight
(less than 5 pounds, 8 ounces).
Every 11 minutes an infant is born at very low birthweight
(less than 3 pounds, 8 ounces).
Every 14 minutes an infant dies in the first year of life.
Every 31 seconds an infant is born to an unmarried mother.
Every 55 seconds an infant is born to a mother who is not a high school graduate.
Every 21 seconds a 15- to 19-year-old woman becomes sexually active for the first time.
Every 32 seconds a 15- to 19-year-old woman becomes pregnant.
Every 64 seconds an infant is born to a teenage mother.
Every 5 minutes an infant is born to a teenage mother who already had a child.
Every 74 seconds a 15- to 19-year-old woman has an abortion.
Every 14 hours a child younger than 5 is murdered.
Every 5 hours a 15- to 19-year-old is murdered.
Every 2 hours a 20- to 24-year-old is murdered.
Every 2 seconds of the school day a public school student is suspended.
Every 4 seconds of the school day a public school student is corporally punished.
Every 10 seconds of the school day a student drops out of school.

Source: Children's Defense Fund (1991). *The State of America's Children*. Washington, D.C.

Schools Need Help

Without doubt, the conditions summarized in these statistics present enormous challenges to public schools, but as Soleil Gregg at the Appalachia Education Lab observes, schools cannot respond effectively without parent and community support:

> Because increasing numbers of children come to school with problems caused by poverty, divorce, drug use, and teenage pregnancy, schools may no longer be able to limit themselves solely to academic roles. Nor can schools act in isolation to overcome such obstacles to learning. Experts agree that schools, families, and communities all share responsibility for children's development and learning.

Gregg's concern is echoed by other educators. Robert Collins Smith, a professor at the University of North Carolina in Chapel Hill, makes a strong case for collaborating with all community entities concerned with the education of children:

> These young people need help from somewhere outside the schools, and the schools need that help in the name of their students....They need a community ready to collaborate and a school that is ready to welcome this collaboration — a school, in short, prepared to find ways to educate all of its students, not just those who come well-rested, well-scrubbed, and culturally and educationally prepared....The job of supporting children to achieve in school and in life is too big a task for families, schools, and community institutions to tackle alone. The whole village has to come together to do the job.

Community ties disappear

Unfortunately, our increasingly mobile, rootless workforce no longer provides the social glue that once held neighborhoods and communities together. Today, strong, lasting community ties are almost impossible to develop. A 1980 survey of high school sophomores found that 36 percent had changed schools at least once since the end of elementary school, and

11 percent had moved three or more times during that period, according to researchers Thomas Hoffer and James Coleman.

American communities have changed in another important respect. Today, fewer than 25 percent of households in many communities have school-age children. Furthermore, the U.S. population is aging rapidly: 30 million people are now over age 65, and this number will increase to 65 million by 2020. Children under 18, who accounted for 34 percent of America's population in 1970, will be 25 percent of the population in 2000, according to Hodgkinson. Finally, immigration rates and ethnic differences in birth rates also are changing the racial and ethnic composition of many communities.

Projections of U.S. Population Age 0-17, 1990-2010 (millions)

Youth	1990	2010	% Change
Total youth*	64.4	64.9	+0.5
White, non-Hispanic	45.2	41.4	-3.8
Hispanic (of any race)	7.2	9.8	+2.6
Black**	10.2	11.4	+1.2
Other races**	2.2	2.8	+0.6
Increase in total nonwhite youth			+4.4 million
Decrease in total white youth			-3.8 million

*May not add exactly because of rounding.
**Includes small number of Hispanics; "other races" are primarily Asian and Native American.

Source: U.S. Census Bureau as cited in National Center for Education Statistics, *Youth Indicators*, Washington, D.C., 1991.

Divided classes

In addition to these social changes, the economic structure of our communities is changing. The "middle" class is shrinking, while the numbers of both rich and poor are growing. Increasingly, America has two workforces: the majority in minimum-wage jobs, with a smaller number in high-paying jobs. As more people recognize poverty as the single factor that holds most children back, these economic changes will present an even greater challenge to schools.

THE LOCAL CHALLENGE

Clearly, these changes in society are unprecedented. No one group has the wherewithal to deal with the myriad problems children face today. Demographer Harold Hodgkinson poses two questions to schools:

- What can educators do that they are not already doing...to get [children] achieving well in a school setting?
- How can educators collaborate more closely with other service providers so they all work together to provide services to children and families?

The key to answering these questions lies in using and redefining the concept of "we." In the context of building learning communities, the "we" is the home, school, and community working together in the framework of a democratic society. The challenge is not to divvy up the responsibilities, but to reconceptualize the role of schools and relationships among the school, the community, and the larger society.

Similarly, Susan McAllister Swap, director of the University of Michigan's Wheelock Center on Families, Communities, Schools, and Children's Learning, sees combining resources as essential to school improvement:

> If the school community honestly commits to the goal of success for all children, then the community also recognizes that the challenge is so great that it cannot be met by parents or teachers or agency personnel working in isolation. The combined resources of the community are essential to discovering and implementing effective solutions to improving public schools.

THE NATIONAL CHALLENGE

In 1990, former President George Bush and the nation's governors met to adopt a national agenda for education reform. The resulting "America 2000" strategy was continued and expanded under the Clinton administration, with the new name "Goals 2000." Interestingly, Goals 2000 added two more goals, with one focused on the importance of parental involvement. This goal reads:

> Every school will promote partnerships that will increase parental involvement and participation in promoting the social, emotional, and academic growth of children.

Robert Collins Smith of the University of North Carolina and others suggest that two things need to happen quickly if there is any hope of accomplishing this and other targets given in Goals 2000:

1. Communities must begin to take responsibility for their children's education, and they must be willing to help schools get students ready to be educated.
2. Schools have to encourage and accept community involvement, believe that all students can be educated, and begin adapting education to the learning styles of these students rather than expecting the students to adapt to a traditional school teaching style.

Why this book?

Clearly, schools have their work cut out for them. This book describes how school systems across the nation are rising to the challenge and seeking new ways to involve parents while strengthening efforts already in place. What it paints is a picture of schools reaching beyond traditional methods, overcoming dread of confrontation and past stereotypes, and leveling bureaucracies for the sake of all children. By depicting school systems at various stages in their programs and services geared toward parental/community collaboration, the authors hope to show that all schools can improve these relationships, however limited the resources at hand.

Chapter 1
The Rationale for Parent and Community Involvement

Not too long ago, many parents and educators shared the opinion that once a child enters school, it is best to leave education to the professionals. After all, the argument went, they are the ones trained to do this job. Besides, the structure of modern curricula is probably too complex for most parents to grasp (remember the New Math?). And what about the parents who can barely read or write — how could they help their children learn anything?

Now we know otherwise. Although our common sense may have whispered it all along, the research has become overwhelmingly clear: parent involvement — and that means all kinds of parents — improves student achievement.

Changing Attitudes

These observations from Anne Henderson, researcher at the National Committee for Citizens in Education, show why parent involvement has become a major component of most school restructuring efforts. Quite simply, research and practice have proven time and again that when parents are involved, children are more successful students.

Parental roles took on heightened status in the 1980s, due in part to the school effectiveness movement, the implementation of site-based management in some schools, school choice, and the growing body of research demonstrating that parent involvement has a significant impact on student achievement.

What the Research Says

From the beginning, the family plays a critical role in helping a child learn to walk, talk, play and interact with others, as well as to develop beliefs, values, attitudes, and the social skills needed to function effectively in society.

According to Paul Barton and Richard Coley of the Educational Testing Service Policy Center:

> There is an intuitive level at which most of us recognize that the basic socializing and nurturing institution is the family — America's smallest school. When we take the time to think about it, it is common sense that the love and attention babies and children receive, the security they feel, the encouragement they get to learn, the intellectual richness of their home environment, and the attention given to their health are all critical in the development of children who are able and motivated to learn.

A 1994 U.S. Department of Education report, "Strong Families, Strong Schools," compiled three decades of research showing a strong correlation between children's learning and family involvement.

"The American family is the rock on which a solid education can and must be built," said Education Secretary Richard Riley.

Important family behaviors

In 1984, based on an extensive review of parent involvement literature, education writer and researcher Rhoda McShane Becher identified "several key family process variables or ways of behaving that are clearly related to student achievement. Children with high achievement scores have parents with high expectations for them, who respond to and interact with them frequently, and who see themselves as teachers of their children." Becher believes that "parent education programs, particularly those training low-income parents to work with their children, are effective in improving how well children use language skills, perform on tests, and behave in school."

Henderson also notes that parental involvement helps not only the children, but also the schools themselves:

The evidence is now beyond dispute: Parent involvement improves student achievement. When parents are involved, children do better in school, and they go to better schools.

Susan McAllister Swap, director of the University of Michigan's Wheelock Center on Families, Communities, Schools, and Children's Learning, writes, "The positive effects of parent involvement on student achievement are sustained across grade levels (preschool through high school), in programs that are home- or school-based, and from programs in low- and middle-income settings." However, parent involvement in low-income settings, while effective in improving student achievement when compared to matched controls, still did not appear to bring achievement scores up to the national level.

Parents want to be informed. Focusing on the effects of school and family partnerships, researchers Joyce Epstein and Karen Salinas, of the Center on Families, Communities, Schools, and Children's Learning at Johns Hopkins University in Baltimore, Maryland, report, "Despite a decline in teachers' practices to involve parents in the upper grades, parents of children at all levels want schools to keep them informed about their children's instructional programs and progress. In short, if guidance is provided, parents of older children will respond."

Epstein, the Center's director, summarizes the results of many researchers' studies over the last decade:

One major message of the early and continuing studies is simply and clearly that families are important for children's learning, development, and school success across the grades. The research suggests that students at all grade levels do better academic work and have more positive attitudes, higher aspirations, and other positive behaviors if they have parents who are aware, knowledgeable, encouraging, and involved.

Reminder: Family Practices That Help Children Succeed

- Students living with both parents have higher proficiency in school, even after controlling for other key factors.
- The more types of reading materials in the home, the better students' reading proficiency.
- Students who do more reading at home are better readers.
- Students who watch a lot of TV have lower academic proficiency.
- The amount of homework done by students has been shown to be positively related to achievement.
- Student absence is directly correlated to decreased academic achievement.
- The amount parents talk about school and assume an active role in school matters is directly correlated to student achievement.
- Income and resources in the home account substantially for children's success in school.

Source: Paul E. Barton and Richard J. Coley, *America's Smallest School*, Educational Testing Service Policy Center, 1992

DO PARENTS WANT TO BE INVOLVED?

The *1992 Phi Delta Kappa/Gallup Poll of the Public's Attitudes Toward the Public Schools* asked respondents if they would be willing to work as unpaid volunteers in the public schools in their communities. More than half the parents said "yes." A related question on the 1993 poll asked how important it was to encourage parents to take a more active part in educating their children. At least 95 percent of all respondents — people with no children in school, public school parents, and non-public school parents — indicated that parent involvement was very important.

A 1993 AASA poll reported similar results: Nearly half the respondents believed requiring parents to volunteer in their school for at least one day each year would be very effective at improving education. Another 46 percent said they would strongly favor a parent volunteer requirement, even if it would raise their taxes.

These results corroborate those of researchers Nancy Feyl Chavkin and David Williams, who studied attitudes toward parent involvement from larger cities in a six-state area — Arkansas, Louisiana, Mississippi, New Mexico, Oklahoma, and Texas. Fifty-nine percent of the respondents were white, and 41 percent were nonwhite. In order of importance, parents indicated they:

1. Wanted to spend time helping their child get the best education.
2. Wanted to cooperate with their child's teacher.
3. Believed they should ensure that their child did homework.
4. Wanted the teacher to give them ideas about how to help their child with reading at home.

Benefits of Home-School Involvement

Based on research and practice, Oliver Moles and Diane D'Angelo of the U.S. Department of Education developed a framework describing the benefits of strong home-school partnerships.

Teachers benefit through:
- Schoolwide training and discussion about how to work effectively with families from diverse backgrounds.
- Support from the principal for their efforts to work with families.
- Tapping the knowledge, skills, and resources of colleagues.
- Maximizing limited resources and time through the cooperative development of grade-level homework and home learning activities.
- A better understanding of parent expectations and closer communication with parents.
- Attaining a higher rate of return on homework and greater involvement of families in home learning activities.
- Increased parental support and cooperation.

Continued on next page

Continued from previous page

Administrators benefit through:
- Better communications between school and home.
- Fewer parent complaints about inconsistent and inappropriate homework.
- Better use of limited resources to address the critical need of linking home and school.
- Improved school climate where children see parents and teachers as partners.

Parents benefit through:
- Opportunities to become partners with teachers and to shape important decisions that enhance their children's chances for success in school.
- Consistent expectations, practices, and messages about homework and home learning activities.
- Increased opportunities to engage in home learning activities with their children.
- Access to schoolwide resources such as parent learning centers, homework hotlines, homework centers, parent workshops, and home visits.

Students benefit through:
- More positive attitudes toward school.
- Higher achievement in reading.
- Higher quality and more grade-appropriate homework.
- Completion of more homework on weekends.
- Observing more similarity between family and school.

WHAT KEEPS SOME PARENTS FROM GETTING INVOLVED?

"Too often, teachers [and administrators and other school personnel] assume that parents who do not actively demonstrate an interest in their child's education are apathetic and unconcerned. This is not always true, however. Chances are these parents want very much to be a part of their child's education, but feel they cannot," writes Pamela Weinberg in her book, *Family Literacy and the School, How Teachers Can Help*. Concerned teachers and administrators will want to find out why some parents feel they cannot get involved and take steps to change their feelings.

In 1989, the Office of Community Education in the Massachusetts Department of Education identified five barriers to parent involvement:

1. **School practices that do not accommodate the growing diversity of families.**
   - Communications to parents are written in languages that may not be appropriate for all families.
   - Schools do not provide parents with information or materials they can use at home to support their children's learning.
   - School staff hold conscious or unconscious attitudes, which may imply that under-involved families do not care about education and have little to add to the school when they do participate.
2. **Time and child care constraints.**
   - Working parents often have difficulty attending daytime school events.
   - Parents may have other child care responsibilities that prevent them from participating in school programs.
3. **Negative experiences with schooling.**
   - Parents whose own school experiences were unsuccessful and stressful may feel uncomfortable in any interaction with their children's school.
   - Young parents who have not finished school may feel uncomfortable about reentering the school setting.
4. **Lack of support for cultural diversity.**
   - Parents with nonmajority cultural and linguistic backgrounds may be uncomfortable in school settings that do not explicitly value the diversity they bring.
   - Linguistic-minority parents who receive only English communications from the school may feel the school does not respect or value their heritage.
   - Parents who have experienced discrimination may feel powerless and alienated from many public institutions, including schools.

5. **Primacy of basic survival needs.**
    - Some families are under extreme pressure from economic stress. The need to provide food, clothing, and shelter takes precedence over involvement in their children's schooling.

More obstacles. Don Davies, director of the Institute for Responsive Education, points out some additional teacher and administrator perceptions and behaviors that discourage involving poor and hard-to-reach parents:

- Children from families that don't conform to middle-class norms often are seen by school officials as having trouble in school.
- Communication between schools and poor families is mostly negative; most of these parents are contacted only when a child is in trouble.
- Teachers and administrators appear to think of poor families as deficient and concentrate on their problems rather than their strengths.
- School staff believe that the problem of "hard-to-reach" parents is the fault of the parents, not the schools.

WHO SHOULD TAKE THE LEAD?

Some education researchers suggest that both parents and educators are responsible when parent involvement is lacking, especially in the case of at-risk students. But Debbie Hamilton and Sandy Osborne of Montana State University believe schools must take the lead if change is to occur:

> Better parent involvement will not just happen. Schools must take the initiative in encouraging parents to become involved. The entire school staff must lead the way in recognizing that education is a partnership of parent-child-teacher. Parents must feel accepted in this partnership. Parents must be free to decide what level of involvement is appropriate for them and have their choice respected. Thus, schools, teachers, and parents cannot afford to blame each

other for problems; they must work together to help each child get the best possible education.

What Practices Encourage Involvement?

Susan Freedman and her colleagues at the Massachusetts Department of Education identified two types of practices that hinder family involvement: school-based and nonschool-based. To correct these practices, they suggest asking the following series of questions about each category.

School-Based Practices:

Communications: Does the school, in its written materials for families, use languages and vocabulary that are easily understood by all parents?

Scheduling of parent events: Is there variety and flexibility in the days, times, and locations of events, so that all parents will have an opportunity to attend at least some events?

Resources and responsibilities: Does anyone in the school have the designated responsibility for reaching out to and making contact with all families? Are there resources behind this commitment? Has the school considered providing child care or transportation — or offering parents who attend school events reimbursement for these expenses?

Attitudes and assumptions: Is there a widespread recognition that teachers and parents are partners with different but parallel roles to play in the education of children? Are the experiences of linguistic and cultural minority parents recognized as rich resources that can enhance the curriculum?

Nonschool-Based Practices:

Employment: Are local employers asked to release family members so they can attend parent-teacher conferences?

Agency contact: What agencies do families use in the community? How could those agencies collaborate to share information on the schools?

Community organizations: Would these organizations be willing to host meetings between parents and representatives of the school? Are there churches, cultural organizations, health centers, and other institutions that have an interest in the families in our schools?

Community resources: Are there ways in which community resources can be used collaboratively to address the training and information needs of parents? Are there ESL and job training classes in the community that may be willing to integrate information on schools in their curriculum?

Chapter 2
Assessing School-Family Relations

School A is on a campaign to involve parents. A new weekly newsletter has been developed that will go home with the children. Parent-teacher nights have been changed to be more flexible to accommodate working and non-English-speaking parents. A family resource coordinator, who has been working with the school for years, has been asked to speak regularly on a local radio talk show.

School B has a small but enthusiastic parent involvement program. The principal is hoping to install more telephones so that teachers may keep parents informed of their children's progress during the day. The local PTA is growing slowly but steadily. Still, the principal feels more can be done, but doesn't quite know where to start.

While School A may be farther along in its parental involvement plan, both schools could benefit from an assessment of their programs that would provide direction and scope — and suggest areas for improvement.

A realistic look. Determining the extent of school-family relations within schools is important for three reasons. First, knowledge of existing efforts or the lack of them provides a needed focus for planning parent and community involvement. Second, identifying problems and needs in these areas enables schools to develop more responsive involvement programs. Third, ongoing assessment allows schools to determine the extent to which long-range programs are succeeding, in addition to providing immediate feedback to guide corrections or adjustments in current efforts.

A Sampling of Surveys and Questionnaires

Questionnaires and surveys are two ways schools can assess their parent/community involvement efforts. They may range in length from one or two pages to complex instruments that take considerable time and resources to complete and tabulate. A sampling of assessment instruments follows.

Taking Stock

Taking Stock, The Inventory of Family, Community, and School Support for Student Achievement is the assessment tool developed in 1993 by the National Committee for Citizens in Education. Adaptable to any school community, this tool introduces the components of an effective family-community-school partnership at both the elementary and secondary levels, helps a school assess how well it is doing in reaching out and working with its community, and shows a school how to use the results to develop a detailed plan for improvement.

Five basic elements form the core of *Taking Stock*:
- Reaching out to families,
- Welcoming families to the school building,
- Developing a strong relationship between families and the school,
- Helping parents understand the school curriculum, and
- Helping parents be more effective as parents and as community members.

Two questionnaires — one for families and one for educators — contain 20 questions each, plus a short series of open-ended questions to help schools and families assess their efforts to work together. Both questionnaires are identical, except that the wording in the family version is more personal, as illustrated in the following examples.

Asked of families:
"Does the school respect and respond to its community's cultural and language differences?"
"Does the school welcome you into the building and make you feel comfortable?"

Asked of educators:
"Does the school make special efforts to reach families of all racial, cultural, and language groups in your community?"
"Does the school welcome parents and family members into the building and make them feel comfortable?"

The basic format of both questionnaires lists the question itself followed by several examples. Respondents are asked to indicate — yes or no — whether their school has the example in place. Then, they're asked to rate their school on the overall topic or area covered in the question.

The process for using *Taking Stock* has three stages: (1) introducing the inventory, interpreting the results, and reporting to the school community; (2) developing an action plan for improving parental involvement; and (3) implementing the plan. It is suggested that a team made up of the principal, teachers, parents, students, and other community members be formed to accomplish each stage. Schools and/or community groups interested in using *Taking Stock* can obtain a notebook that includes directions and all the materials needed for completing the three stages. The *Taking Stock* process is outlined on the next page.

For more information, contact the Center for Law and Education, 1875 Connecticut Ave. NW, Washington, DC 20009; (202) 462-7688.

Overview of the *Taking Stock* Process

Stage 1: Introducing *Taking Stock*, interpreting results, and reporting to community (3-6 weeks)

1. Select survey team (5-10 people)

- Principal
- Parents
- Teachers
- Other staff
- Students

2. Present *Taking Stock* to the community

- Publicize *Taking Stock*
- Hold gatherings for families and educators:
  - Explain *Taking Stock*
  - Answer questions
  - Give survey
  - Hold discussion

3. Interpret and report on the results

- Tally surveys
- Compile "Last Words"
- Score and interpret findings
- Draft and present a short report to school community

Stage 2: Developing an action plan (4-6 weeks)

4. Select action team (15-20 people)

- Principal/administrator
- Parents
- Teachers
- Other staff
- Students
- Community representatives

5. Develop draft action plan

- Review findings and report
- Set priorities (Chapter 8)
- Consult:
  - Steps to success
  - Troubleshooting
  - On Balance
  - Parents in Action
- Draft action plan for each priority

6. Obtain approval of action plan

- Circulate action plan draft:
  - Parent groups
  - Teachers association/union
  - School staff
  - Community groups
  - District staff
- Finalize action plan
- Publicize action plan

Stage 3: Implementing the action plan (1-2 years)

7. Select Family-School Partnership Task Force

- Principal/administrator
- Parent representatives/parents
- Teacher representatives/teachers
- Community representatives / local citizens and community groups

8. Form subcommittees

- Assign tasks
- Set timeliness
- Meet/discuss progress
- Report to task force

9. Evaluate progress and revise action plan

- Report to:
  - Parent groups
  - School staff
  - Community groups
  - District staff
  - School board
  - Public

10. Re-do *Taking Stock*

The Johns Hopkins questionnaires

Over the past several years, the Center for Families, Communities, Schools, and Children's Learning at Johns Hopkins University in Baltimore, Maryland, has developed a series of questionnaires called *School and Family Partnerships: Surveys*. Designed for research and improving practice, this series has questionnaires for teachers and parents at the elementary, middle school, and high school levels.

The teacher questionnaires ask for their judgments about parent involvement, the practices they currently are using, and what partnership programs they would like to see developed in the school and in their own classrooms. Parent questionnaires focus on attitudes toward the school, how parents currently are involved, how the school asks them to be involved, and what partnership programs they would like to see improved or started. All forms include requests for basic demographic information and several open-ended questions so that respondents can provide opinions and give suggestions. The parent questionnaires can be completed in 15-20 minutes and the teacher questionnaires in 20-25 minutes.

The questionnaires come with a guide, "How To Summarize Your School's Survey Data," that explains how to develop basic descriptive statistics on the results. More sophisticated analyses also are possible.

For more information, contact the Johns Hopkins Center on Families, Schools, and Children's Learning, 3505 N. Charles St., Baltimore, MD 21218; (410) 516-8800.

PTA questionnaires

The National Parent Teacher Association has a two-page questionnaire that parents or school personnel can use "to assess the amount of parent involvement individuals feel exists now and what they feel to be a desirable level of participation." The 20 questions are easily scored and interpreted. For parents, low scores indicate they believe schools should handle education decisions and are uncertain about whether parents should be involved. Higher scores from parents indicate they want to help make school decisions and are highly motivated to get involved. Low scores for school personnel suggest that they question the value of parent involvement, while higher scores mean that school personnel are more open to having parents involved.

Alabama's Plan for Excellence

A Plan for Excellence: Alabama's Public Schools Parental Involvement Plan is an example of a state-developed assessment tool that includes two instruments for parents. One allows parents to rate their schools on several aspects and to identify various strengths and weaknesses. A teacher survey with five open-ended questions asks teachers to identify ways that parents might help in the school and to list any anticipated problems with parent involvement. A "Checklist for Parental Involvement," another part of the plan, provides schools with a mechanism for assessing the current status of parent involvement, including a determination of how many parents are involved.

For more information, contact the communications division, Alabama Department of Education, Gordon Persons Office Building, 50 N. Ripley St., Montgomery, AL 36120-3901; (205) 242-9705.

Florida's "Red Carpet Schools" Campaign

Annually, Florida's Public Education Awareness Committee, made up of members of the Sunshine State School Public Relations Association and representatives of the Department of Education, develops a public relations campaign to direct positive attention to some aspect of education in the state. The 1990 focus was family involvement, with the goal of promoting "a family-school alliance to enhance student success."

The campaign had two phases. Phase One targeted educators, focusing on their training and awareness to ensure a friendly, welcoming atmosphere. Phase Two targeted family members, focusing on recruitment.

Phase One's theme — "Red Carpet Schools: Families Welcome!" — was a tool to motivate substantive changes in school employee attitudes, programs, and facilities. To communicate that parents are indeed welcome, each school district was asked to form steering committees to direct local campaign efforts. Schools had to meet certain criteria to be eligible for the Red Carpet designation. A parent group within the school nominates schools for Red Carpet designation, after working with staff to investigate the criteria, and answers the following 11 questions about school-family relations:

1. Have you conducted a random survey to determine family attitudes?
2. Are your physical facilities responsive to and available to family and community?
   - Are directions clear and simple for getting to your office?
   - Upon entering the office, is there a warm and friendly reception area, including a place for visiting parents to sit?
3. Is a friendly, welcoming atmosphere created by your entire staff?
   - Do those who answer phones in your school receive training?
   - Are all staff members (including custodians, food service workers, and paraprofessionals) trained to be welcoming?
4. Do you provide opportunities for parenting education?
   - Do staff members and parents have opportunities to work together for the benefit of children?
   - For example, do schools offer classes or topic sessions on discipline, communication, motivation, study skills, or homework?

5. Do you provide opportunities for family involvement in the learning process?
   - Is curriculum broken down and explained to parents, giving them ways to help their children?
   - For instance, are families provided with calendars listing daily activities, and curriculum fairs? Do counselors explain to parents course requirements, four-year plans, and substance abuse prevention?
6. Do you have a parent/community group participating in an advisory function in your school?
   - Does a parent/community group participate in preparing your school's annual report, determining needs of the school, and reviewing the school's budget?
7. Do you have scheduled formal opportunities for parent and community visitations?
   - For instance, do you have open houses, community days, or career days?
8. Do you produce a periodic publication for family and community?
   - For instance, are newsletters, weekly menus, homework folders, and school calendars sent home?
9. Do you have a system of ongoing personal communication between the school (teacher) and the family?
   - Are phone calls or home visits encouraged?
   - Do teachers meet with parents at times other than when a student is in trouble?
   - Are happy-grams, letters, conferences, and written notes used?
10. Are family and the community involved in general goal setting?
    - Do you solicit opinions on decisions dealing with school facilities, programs, equipment, and needs?
11. Are you sensitive to and do you accommodate families of students with special needs?

A starting point. These are just a few examples of existing questionnaires schools and school districts may want to look at when developing their own assessments. As these models show, it is important to hear both sides of the story by asking the same or similar questions of both schools and parents. In some cases, answers that vary greatly may point out some misperceptions that, when cleared up, could go a long way in improving relationships.

These examples also illustrate many of the areas important to fostering good relationships, such as open and friendly facilities, trained staff, communications vehicles, and family resource personnel on school staffs.

Building solid parent/school relationships is a matter of taking a multipronged approach. But to make the first steps toward improvement, a district must know where it stands in relation to available opportunities for solidifying home, school, and community.

Chapter 3
A Framework for Parent Involvement

Schools have many different ways of dealing with parents and fostering parental and community involvement. Some of these ways are deeply ingrained, based on individual personalities of school leaders, teachers and others, or perhaps on negative or positive past experiences.

While most schools say they are doing everything they can to involve parents, the reality is that some dread the prospect of more parental involvement and actually adopt a protective stance that does little to welcome parents into the school halls. Although feelings of defensiveness may be perfectly justified, the practice of holding tight to school control and keeping parents at a distance goes against what we now know is good for student achievement and success in school.

Four Models of Parent Involvement

In 1993, Susan McAllister Swap, a researcher and education writer at the University of Michigan, suggested parent involvement efforts follow four basic models: protective, school-to-home transmission, curriculum enrichment, and partnership. In *Developing Home-School Partnerships: From Concepts to Practice*, she describes the assumptions, advantages, and disadvantages of each model.

In the **protective model** the goals are to reduce conflict between parents and educators, primarily by separating their functions, and to protect the school from parent interference. The assumptions are that parents delegate to the school the responsibility of educating their children, that they hold school personnel accountable for results, and that educators accept this responsibility.

This model has the advantage of effectively protecting the school against parental intrusion in most circumstances. On the other hand, it exacerbates home-school conflicts by failing to create any structure or predictable opportunities for preventive problem solving. The protective model also ignores the potential of home-school collaboration for improving student achievement and rejects potential resources for enrichment and school support that could be available from families and other community members.

In the **school-to-home transmission model**, the goal is to enlist parent support for school objectives. It assumes that children's achievement is fostered by continuity of expectations and values between home and school. This model also assumes that parents emphasize the importance of schooling, reinforce school expectations at home, provide home conditions that support school success, and ensure their child meets minimum academic and social requirements.

Programs based on the transmission model have been known to increase children's school success. In order to work, however, school personnel should identify and communicate the values and practices outside the school that contribute to school success. This leads to one advantage of the transmission model: Parents get clear direction from the school about the social and academic skills their children need for success and about their role in developing those skills. In most cases, parents welcome this clear transmission of information, and it is helpful to parents outside the social mainstream, such as those who do not speak English, have little contact with the school, or fall into one of the at-risk categories for families.

However, programs built on the transmission model may reflect a school's unwillingness to consider parents as equal partners with important strengths. Schools often find it difficult to draw clear boundaries between the roles of school and home in formal education and may, in the effort to transmit the school's values and goals, demean the value and importance of the family's culture. This model also ignores the facts that some parents cannot devote a lot of time and energy to parent involvement activities, and that differences in class or educational background can make both teachers and parents feel uncomfortable and threatened.

In the **curriculum enrichment model**, the goal is to

expand and extend the school's curriculum by incorporating family contributions. Like the transmission model, it assumes a continuity of learning, with home and school working together to enrich curriculum objectives and content. Also, the relationship between home and school is based on mutual respect — both parents and teachers are seen as experts and resources in the process of discovery. This model draws on parents' knowledge and expertise to increase the resources available to the school, and it provides rich opportunities for adults to learn from each other. The contributions of immigrant or minority families who traditionally have not participated in schools are especially welcomed.

Investment is great. However, the curriculum enrichment model demands a significant investment of parents' and educators' time, resources, support, and study. Further, the number of different cultures represented in some classrooms makes curricular adaptation very complex. This model also ignores the ongoing debate about the school's mission in educating children with diverse backgrounds — should a "majority culture" be taught to all or should student diversity be reflected and valued in the curriculum? In this model, too, differences in class or educational background can make teachers and parents feel uncomfortable and threatened.

In the **partnership model**, the primary goal is to get parents and educators working together to accomplish a common mission: academic success for all children. Accomplishing this mission requires both groups to re-envision the school environment and create new policies, practices, structures, roles, relationships, and attitudes to realize the vision. It also demands collaboration among parents, members of the community, and educators. This task requires many resources, so none of these groups is likely to accomplish it independently.

An advantage of this model is that it establishes a true partnership for transforming the vision of school culture based on collegiality, experimentation, mutual support, and joint problem solving. But to implement the partnership model, the traditionally isolated educator's role must be exchanged for a collaborative one. New patterns of scheduling and interaction are needed to support this new role. A leader who is a facilitator and a "cheerleader" also is essential, along with school and district policies to support the collaboration.

THEORY TO PRACTICE

The following pages highlight some successful parent involvement models in school districts across the country.

The Cherry Creek partnership model

Cherry Creek School District Number 5 in Englewood, Colorado, has a broad-based program for parent involvement. According to Brenda Holben, prevention coordinator, "Cherry Creek believes that parent-family involvement boosts student achievement, encourages parents to volunteer in school programs, creates an advocacy for parents, involves parents in governance, and builds partnership between school and community. The district encourages parents to volunteer in school programs, involves parents in governance, and builds partnerships between school and community."

The Cherry Creek model is implemented through several programs and activities:

- **Parent Council.** A partnership of 40 parent-teacher organizations, including PTO presidents, school principals, other school administrators, and school board members, meets monthly to discuss important district issues. This council is a communication vehicle for parents, teachers, administrators, community members, and the board of education.
- **Parent Information Network (PIN).** Each school has a PIN representative on the PTA board. Representatives meet monthly to hear speakers on issues facing students and families in the community. The PIN plans and implements programs to meet the needs of students, staff, families, and community at individual school buildings.

The group's goals are to:
— Determine problems and explore the child's environment.
— Gather and share information.
— Monitor legislation.
— Review curriculum offerings.
— Offer parenting programs and coordinate school-parent programs.
— Provide educational programs for youth, parents, and the community so that all are better able to deal with today's choices.

- **Cherry Creek Schools' Foundation.** Established in the spring of 1993, the foundation provides a vehicle for the private sector and individuals to invest in public education. The 501(c)3 organization promotes supplemental and alternative funding opportunities that expand resources to enhance educational programs for students with basic needs and other student enrichment programs. The foundation also supports efforts to implement new technological applications linking homes to schools.

Collaboration and partnership also are important aspects of the Cherry Creek School District's efforts. These efforts include:

- **Community Prevention Project, Inc.** A collaborative community-school group providing funds for employing the prevention coordinator, who directs the federal Drug-Free Schools and Community Act grant. This coordinator is responsible for planning and implementing drug abuse prevention strategies and training programs in the district.

- **Alternative to Suspension Parent/Student Program.** A program designed to work with first-time student offenders who violate the district's drug and alcohol policy. Violators and their parents are required to attend a 2½ hour workshop presented in partnership with the Young Lawyers Association and the local medical association.

- **Family-School-Community Liaison.** A group of parent liaisons from nine district schools, funded by a combination of school funds, community investments, and a grant from the

Drug-Free Schools and Community Act. The objectives of the liaisons are to:
— Provide information about community resources.
— Encourage parents to become involved in their children's education.
— Provide effective and alternative parenting strategies.
— Foster communication among the school, families, and the community.
— Develop skills and attitudes among parents that will help them assure their children's success in school.

• **Summit.** During the spring of 1993, nearly 500 community and staff volunteers participated in a series of focus groups to rethink and redefine education for the Cherry Creek School District. New realities facing the schools were addressed and a future course was plotted.

For more information on Cherry Creek's programs, contact Brenda Holben, prevention coordinator, Cherry Creek School District No. 5, 4700 S. Yosemite St., Englewood, CO 80111 (303) 486-4247

Florida's "Family/School/Community Partnership" model

The Family/School/Community Partnership Program, a model for strengthening families, is a collaborative effort of the vocational home economics education staff of the Florida Department of Education and Florida State University. Family education programs, materials, and home-school-community partnerships are designed to incorporate six family strengths:

• **Commitment:** Nurturing a special kind of caring that is consistent and constant. In a special activity, parents and children signed a contract not to watch television for a specific time period. As part of their contract, parents agreed to provide a replacement activity in which they participated with the child, such as reading. At the end of the period, a celebration was planned.

- **Appreciation:** Affirming the support family members provide. Throughout the year, little "I Appreciate You" notes are sent to teachers, students, and parents, sometimes anonymously. An end-of-the-year appreciation luncheon and ceremony is held for all teachers.
- **Communication:** Encouraging and supporting family members who are good listeners and who communicate respect, reciprocity, emotional intimacy, and positive responses. Schools hold "Report Card Pick-Ups," where parents pick up their child's report card and have an opportunity to talk with teachers. Parents are not required to come to the school to pick up the report cards, but it is expected. In 1992-93, 98 percent of the parents participated.
- **Time Together:** Providing opportunities for sharing, fun, and humor among schools, students, and families. To create a feeling of "school family," schools held a two-day overnight orientation retreat for all ninth-graders. On the second day, family members joined the teachers and students for a cookout to get to know each other better.
- **Family Wellness:** Sharing values, goals, and priorities and developing self-esteem, autonomy, moral and ethical sensitivity, traditions, and intergenerational respect. Schools held evening programs on parent needs, such as parent education, support groups, and money management.
- **Management of Resources, Crises, and Stress:** Uniting parents, schools, and students to deal with problems, cope with losses, and take risks. During a recent student crisis, the school called in a group of parents — not necessarily the parents of the students involved. They served as student mentors during a day-long session where students could talk things out and resolve differences.

Florida's program makes the school the change catalyst. The school mobilizes the community to create partnerships where community resources are used to strengthen families. The partnerships must be reciprocal — for teachers and administrators to support parents, parents must be willing to communicate with school personnel and commit to working with them. Likewise, the community must begin to accept responsibility for supporting and caring for all its children. The workplace must become "family-friendly," enabling individuals to balance work and family.

The Family/School/Community Partnership Program has two primary components:

1. **Family education.** The heart of the program, it provides programs and activities for developing healthy, nurturing, supportive families. Integrating family concepts into all curricula, kindergarten through postsecondary, is key to the program's success. Activities involving students, teachers, families, and community members emphasize information sharing and help the family create a supportive home learning environment.
2. **Community partnerships.** This function ensures that community support services needed by children and families are provided efficiently and effectively, with minimal disruptions. Activities are geared toward prevention, early intervention, support, and outreach. They include maintaining a Family Resource Center, which helps families and educators locate useful information and provide support services when needed.

For more information, contact Mildred Alexander, FSC School Program Director, Florida State University, P.O. Box 3025 FSU, Tallahassee, FL 32306; (904) 644-6426.

Jefferson Foundation partnership model

The Jefferson Foundation in Golden, Colorado, was established in 1983 as a partnership of leaders from education, the private sector, and the Jefferson County community. Its mission is to develop and fund programs that expand educational opportunities for students and to sponsor improvement in the overall quality of public education. Encouraging parent involvement is one part of the foundation's comprehensive efforts.

Since 1989, the Jefferson Foundation has worked with the Jefferson County Public Schools community and the school district to implement the recommendations of Education 2000, a two-year study by more than 300 citizens and educators.

The recommendations include:

- **Implement a system of site-based management and shared decision making to increase involvement and achievement.** Teams of students, teachers, parents, support staff, administrators, and community members learned to work together during a foundation-sponsored leadership academy in 1993. They defined leadership roles in the school, coordinated community priorities, resolved differences, and made decisions for their individual schools. The foundation continues to support these teams as they work to guide their schools to meet the challenges of the 21st century.

- **Increase community involvement to promote ownership and enhance opportunities for students.** The Foundation received a Danforth Grant in 1993 to support the first year of its "Total Quality Services: Transforming a Community" project. The effort uses a systemic approach and the philosophy of total quality management to restructure the delivery of educational and other human services to better serve students and their families. Initial activities included establishing a Coordinating Council for Quality, an Internal Support Transition Team, and a leadership conference involving all of the district administrators and representatives of employee organizations, parent groups, the Colorado Alliance of Business, and social service agencies.

- **Strengthen communications to enhance understanding.** In 1992, three elementary schools received foundation grants to research strategies for enhancing home-school communication through trust and shared responsibility for children's learning. Pennington Elementary employed a home-school liaison to work with at-risk children and their families. Parenting classes and family-based learning activities were conducted.

Sheridan Green Elementary targets children and their families for whom English is a second language. Stein Elementary developed an Early Start program to equip preschool children and their families with skills children need to be successful in school.

For more information, contact Cherie Lyons, executive director, Jefferson Foundation, 1829 Denver West Dr., Golden, CO 80401; (303) 273-6834.

TYPES OF PARENT INVOLVEMENT

Parent involvement is a many-faceted concept. Schools and school districts usually take different approaches to bringing parents into the school community on various levels.

Erwin Flaxman and Morton Inger of the ERIC Clearinghouse on Urban Education at Teachers College, Columbia University, classify three types of parent involvement: (1) direct involvement in the school, (2) parent training programs, and (3) family resource and support programs.

With direct involvement, parents and schools mutually benefit by working together to enlighten parents and get work done at the school. Efforts might include school choice programs, site-based management, local school councils, and various types of school volunteer activities.

Parent training programs usually are intended to help parents develop communication skills to work more effectively with their children. Two well-known commercial programs of this type are Parent Effectiveness Training (PET) and Systematic Training for Effective Parenting (STEP). More recent programs have added long-term parent support to "strengthen parents' own desires to do what is best for their children and try to build parents' self-esteem...particularly in their abilities as learners and teachers," according to Flaxman and Inger.

Family resource and support programs affect what happens to children before and after school, in the home, the neighborhood, and the community. These programs usually provide direct services such as home visits, health care, drug and alcohol treatment, child care for working parents, and a referral system to other social services.

Another perspective

Anne Henderson of the National Committee for Citizens in Education also classified three similar approaches to parent involvement: (1) improving the parent-child relationship, (2) bringing parents into the school, and (3) building a partnership between home and school.

Improving the parent-child relationship. Some educators believe that improving parent-child relationships may require interceding in the home learning environment. This is based on the premise that "building a strong learning environment at home — including holding high expectations of success and encouraging positive attitudes toward education — powerfully affects student achievement," Henderson said.

The school's role is three-fold — encouraging parents to work with their children, providing information to parents, and helping parents develop the skills needed to work with their children at home.

Home-school centers, sometimes called parent education centers, are one way of assisting families in their basic obligations. In the centers, schools offer parents a wealth of resources about parenting and child-rearing concerns. Many centers offer both written and audiovisual materials. In Fairfax County, Virginia, where more than 75 languages are spoken in the public schools, the Parenting Education Center has written resources available in nine languages and tapes in four languages. Topics range from school issues, such as homework and parent involvement, to family and child development issues, such as discipline, communication, television viewing, and dealing with stress. The center also identifies community resources for parents.

Many home-school centers also provide parenting classes at schools or other locations throughout the community. Typically, class topics are age- or problem-specific, which makes for natural peer and support groups among the attending parents.

In Fairfax County, the topics include childbirth/parenthood preparation, the young child/school-age child/adolescent child, and general parenting. A number of courses are offered within each subject area. For example, classes offered under the topic of the young child include "As Baby Grows," "Toilet Training," "Friendly Discipline for Preschoolers," "Taming the TV Monster," and "Siblings Without Rivalry."

Many home-school centers have personnel who are available to lecture before community groups on topics of specific interest. The intent in all these activities is to help parents better carry out their task of raising healthy children who are ready to learn.

For more information on Fairfax County's center, contact Nancy Scesney, program specialist, Parenting Education Center, Fairfax County Public Schools, 7510 Lisle Ave., Falls Church, VA 22043; (703) 506-2221.

Bringing parents into the school. In the Henderson model, two examples of this approach are parents who volunteer both in and outside of classrooms and parents who work in schools as paid aides. These practices not only improve students' academic achievement and attitudes, but also have a positive effect on the parents and teachers.

"Parents developed better attitudes toward schools and school staff members, helped gather support in the community, became more active in community affairs, and sought more education for themselves," said Henderson. She also noted "teachers devoted more time to teaching, were more likely to experiment, and developed approaches that were more student-oriented."

Parent Volunteers

In Blytheville, Arkansas, the educational philosophy is that everyone must work together to provide a worthwhile program for all students. The public schools have a strong volunteer program that includes the PTA, Partners in Education, Volunteers in Public School, various steering committees, and coaches for Odyssey of the Mind (an academic competition program).

An excerpt from one of the school newsletters describes the importance of volunteers in education:

> They build ant farms for an elementary school science class. They enrich the already fertile imaginations of Odyssey of the Mind competitors. They give the sobering facts about drug abuse. They adopt rooms full of students as their own. They supervise the playgrounds at recess. They provide supplies, establish scholarships, raise money, plan events, judge contests.
>
> Most of all, they share. They are the volunteers who have allowed Blytheville Public Schools to offer a well-rounded education that is grounded in the basics and enhanced by the "extras" such as band, academic competitions, and exposure to the arts. Volunteers from business and industry are at the heart of a Partners in Education program that has become a model for neighboring districts because of the breadth and scope of its activities. Civic clubs, church groups, colleges, and the city Police and Fire Departments are a part of this effort. These volunteers have set the example for tomorrow's leaders, who one day will carry on their legacy of service.

For more information, contact M. Janet Taylor, assistant superintendent, Blytheville Public Schools, 200 S. Lake St., Blytheville, AR 72315; (501) 762-2053.

Building a partnership between home and school.
Henderson's third approach focuses on well-planned, comprehensive, long-term efforts to involve parents and the family in a variety of school roles and to work with parents to strengthen their role as teachers at home.

Parent centers — sometimes called family centers — are a relatively new example of this approach. In her study of 28 centers in 14 states, Vivian Johnson of the Johns Hopkins Center on Families, Communities, Schools, and Children's Learning found that all but two were started in the last five years. Unlike parent information centers, which usually are initiated by the school or district to provide a range of information, family centers often are initiated by parents in consultation with principals and teachers to serve a particular school. Parent centers are specific places where parents and other family members meet, plan, and implement programs that they initiate or develop cooperatively with school staff. A distinguishing feature of family centers is that they frequently are the support place in schools where everyone feels welcome because the school hierarchy doesn't interfere with relationships. As Johnson points out:

> In providing a space for parents that is their own place to come and go as they determine, educators are symbolically changing the role of parents from outsiders (invited guests) to insiders (members of the team). No longer are parents asked to come to schools only for special occasions like open house or performances of their children. Rather, parents are asked to join in the process of education by tutoring, monitoring lessons, accompanying field trips, planning activities, and governing schools. Teachers remain school professionals, but parents are more and more frequently asked to become collaborators in the schooling process.

Making Parents the Focus

Researchers Judith Vandegrift and Andrea Greene in 1992 evaluated parent involvement programs in 55 primary and secondary schools in Arizona. From this evaluation, they developed the four-part matrix pictured below, which categorizes involvement from the perspectives of support and participation.

In Vandegrift and Greene's matrix, the focus is on parents and whether or not they are active or inactive, supportive or not supportive. The authors believe this approach is a realistic means for developing a parent involvement effort; a key element is that it allows schools to design a program based on the interests and needs of parents.

Four Types of Parents

+ Supportive of child (for example, often encourages) + Active participant (for example, helps child with homework)	− Not supportive of child (for example, ignores child) + Active participant (for example, comes if food is provided)
+ Supportive of child (for example, cares for well-being) − Inactive participant (for example, rarely comes to school activities)	− Not supportive of child (for example, is abusive) − Inactive participant (for example, no communication with school)

A SAMPLING OF INVOLVEMENT DESIGNS

Numerous designs have been developed for parent and community involvement programs. Several of the more widely recognized programs are described in this section. These programs should serve as a reference point for schools interested in initiating a new program or in expanding an existing effort.

National Committee for Citizens in Education

Education researchers Anne Henderson, Carl Marburger and Theodora Ooms of the National Committee for Citizens in Education outline five basic roles that parents can play in their children's education: partners, collaborators and problem solvers, audience members, supporters and advisors, and co-decision makers.

Parents as partners. As their children get older, parents move from being the prime educator to sharing this role with the schools.

At this stage, much of the parent role relates to the legal responsibility to enroll a child in school. Parents are expected to register their child; obtain the required vaccinations and medical exams; purchase necessary supplies; respond to school communications; and ensure their child is properly dressed, gets to school on time, and attends each day. In addition, parents have certain rights, including access to school records, due process in discipline and other issues, and involvement in decisions about special education placement.

Parents as collaborators and problem solvers. Parents can encourage and reward satisfactory achievement, show interest in their child's school day, and enforce policies about bedtime, television, and homework. They also can provide enrichment activities that reinforce school learning, including reading to the child, making library or museum trips, and participating in a variety of other home or community activities. When a child is having difficulty at school, parents may be asked by the school to help solve the problem; it may take substantial negotiation between home and school before it is resolved.

Parents as audience. Parents are encouraged to attend activities and events designed to draw them into the school. These include open houses, back-to-school nights, athletic events, concerts, and plays. A major purpose of these events is to inform parents in a direct, personal way. Also, children usually feel good when they see their parents in the audience at a school function.

Parents as supporters. Parents volunteer to help in their own child's or in other classrooms, work in the school library, tutor special-needs children, make attendance phone calls, or share their expertise in enrichment programs. Parent-teacher organizations provide opportunities for parents to become involved in other supportive activities, as do parent education programs and parent support networks.

Parents as advisors and co-decision makers. This role is most often accomplished through some type of parent advisory group. Other possibilities, which move toward real power sharing, include positions on elected school governing boards and councils developed as part of site-based management efforts.

The National Committee for Citizens in Education has been dissolved, but publications and resources are available from the Center for Law and Education (see Resources).

Center on Families, Communities, Schools, and Children's Learning

Joyce Epstein of the Johns Hopkins University Center on Families, Communities, Schools, and Children's Learning in Baltimore, Maryland, developed the following parent involvement typology to "help families and schools fulfill their shared responsibilities for children's learning and development." The categories are:

Type 1: Basic Obligations of Families. Parent responsibilities for their child's health, safety, and school readiness. Development of a positive home situation that supports learning throughout the child's school years.

Type 2: Basic Obligations of Schools. Schools communicate with parents through notices, phone calls, home visits, report cards, newsletters, and parent-teacher conferences. Two-way communication strengthens the partnership between parents and the school.

Type 3: Involvement at School. Parents volunteer in the school, and families come to the school to attend various events.

Type 4: Learning Activities at Home. Parents are encouraged to work with children at home to support classwork or advance and enrich learning.

Type 5: Involvement in Decision Making, Governance, and Advocacy. Along with other community members, parents participate as members of advisory councils, school-site management teams, PTA/PTO groups, and other school committees. Parents also may become involved with independent advocacy groups in the community.

Type 6: Collaboration with Community Organizations. Schools encourage collaboration with other community agencies that share responsibility for children's education. Possibilities include organizations that provide before- and after-school child care, health services, social services, and cultural activities. Schools also help parents access resources to improve home conditions.

Positive Outcomes Linked to Each Type of Parent Involvement

Parent Outcomes

Type 1. Parenting
Self-confidence in parenting
Knowledge of child development
Understanding of home as environment for learning

Type 2. Communicating
Understanding of school programs
Interacting with school faculty and staff
Monitoring child's progress

Type 3. Volunteering
Understanding teacher's job and school program
Becoming familiar with teachers and school personnel
Increasing comfort in interactions at school

Type 4. Learning at Home
Interaction with child as student at home
Support and encouragement of school work
Participation in child's education

Type 5. Representing Other Parents
Input to policies that affect child's educaton
Feeling in control of environment

Type 6. Collaboration
Solving problems usually associated with community school relations
Increased knowledge about community services

Student Outcomes

Type 1. Parenting
Security
Respect for parent
continued on next page

Improved attendance
Awareness of importance of school
Type 2. Communicating
Student participation in parent-teacher conferences or in preparation for conferences
Better decisions about courses and programs
Type 3. Volunteering
Increased learning skills from receiving individual attention
Greater ease of communication with adults
Type 4. Learning at Home
Homework completion
Improved confidence in ability as learner
Greater achievement in skills practices
Type 5. Representing Other Parents
Rights protected
Specific benefits linked to specific policies
Type 6. Collaboration
Make connections with other community resources
Help avoid fragmented and duplicated services

Teacher Outcomes
Type 1. Parenting
Understanding of distinct family cultures, goals, talents, and needs
Type 2. Communicating
Knowledge that family has common base of information for discussion of student problems and progress
Use of parent network for communications
Type 3. Volunteering
Awareness of parent interest in school and children and parent willingness to help
Readiness to try programs that involve parents in many ways
Feeling of parent support for programs
Type 4. Learning at Home
Respect and appreciation for parents' time and ability to follow through and influence learning
Better design of homework assignments
Type 5. Representing Other Parents
Equal status interaction with parents to improve school programs
Awareness of parent perspectives for policy development
Type 6. Collaboration
Share responsibility for young people's education and their future success
Better distribution of service

Source: Adapted from Epstein, J. (1992). "School and Family Partnerships," *Encyclopedia of Educational Research*. New York, NY: MacMillan.

Institute for Responsive Education

The Institute, located in Boston, Massachusetts, has developed a national project called the League of Schools Reaching Out, which focuses on three themes: providing success for all children, serving the whole child, and sharing responsibility. Beginning in 1989 with two demonstration schools, the League of Schools Reaching Out grew to involve 41 elementary and middle schools in 19 urban school districts in 1991. "The League subscribes to no single orthodoxy, but its members share a commitment to the three themes sketched above," said Don Davies, the Institute's director.

The Schools Reaching Out project proposes an easily adaptable three-part strategy based on what has worked in the demonstration schools. The first strategy is to create a parent center to provide space for parents within a school. The center serves as a focal point for many activities organized by and for parents, and teachers and administrators also may use it as a resource center.

The demonstration schools also had success with using school staff as home visitors. These individuals "were not social workers or truant officers. They provided information to families about school expectations, the curriculum, rules and requirements, and they dispensed advice and materials on how family members could help children with their school work," Davies said.

Other roles for home visitors include agency referrals for needed services and listening to family members' concerns and needs, which can then be shared with teachers. An important aspect of the home visitor program is the visitor's working relationship with teachers. Home visitors must be seen as colleagues who can provide valuable information and assistance to teachers and administrators as they work with children in the school.

The project's third strategy involves developing action research teams of teachers. According to Davies, the teams' purpose is "to involve teachers directly in studying home/school/community relations and in devising actions to improve their own practice." Teams operate under the premise that change and improvement are more likely if teachers work together to find solutions to problems, have time for reflection, and are supported for trying out new strategies.

New ways to define involvement. As a result of experiences gained in these schools and the data gathered by the researchers involved, new and broader definitions of parent involvement are being explored. The new definitions include a focus on:

- The whole family rather than on just parents,
- Inclusion of all child-serving agencies and institutions,
- Inclusion of home and neighborhood activities and services,
- Efforts to involve families that are traditionally considered "hard to reach,"
- Inclusion of families' priorities as well as those of teachers and administrators, and
- Family strengths rather than deficits.

The Center for Collaborative Education

A New York City network of staff- and parent-run schools, the Center has at its core a group of Central Park East schools developed by Deborah Meier and her colleagues over the past two decades. Meier is co-director of Central Park East Secondary School. The schools serve predominately poor and minority students. School organization emphasizes choice, active learning, collaborative and interdisciplinary teaching, alternative assessment, a multicultural curriculum, and individualized instruction that tries to eliminate tracking and other discriminatory practices. Parents play key roles on school governance teams that decide policy in all areas. The Center is the New York City affiliate of the Coalition of Essential Schools, developed by Ted Sizer and his colleagues at Brown University.

Norm Fruchter, Anne Galletta, and J. Lynne White of the Academy for Educational Development in Washington, D.C., observe that both the League of Schools Reaching Out and the Center for Collaborative Education were initiated and implemented by university-based scholar-activists working as external collaborators with individual schools and school systems. Both programs have a variety of components, including parent involvement, designed to restructure schools and improve academic achievement, and both depend more on the participating schools' commitment than on specific strategies.

Home and School Institute

The Home and School Institute (HSI) of Washington, D.C., has focused on parent involvement programs since its founding in 1965. HSI emphasizes the importance of the family role in education and works to promote partnerships among the complex forces that affect education today. HSI has developed staff training programs and special curricula in such areas as "home-based learning, services for the handicapped child, multicultural programs, and cross-generational approaches to child rearing," according to Dorothy Rich, the Institute's director, and her colleague Beverly Mattox. The HSI parent involvement goals are to:

1. Enable all families to assist children in advancing their educational achievement.
2. Offer curriculum and training programs that enable schools and community organizations to provide a tutoring role for families.
3. Reach wide numbers of families effectively and efficiently.

MegaSkills is HSI's framework for parent involvement. Rich, creator of MegaSkills, says, "It is generally agreed that children need certain basic skills (usually called the three R's) in order to succeed. But for children to learn and keep learning basic skills at school, they need to learn another important set of basics at home." Rich describes "MegaSkills" as "long-lasting, achievement-enhancing skills....[They are] what makes possible the use of the other skills that we learn." According to Rich, the family can teach a child these skills before the child attends school and can continue to reinforce them once school has started.

A MegaSkills Education Center was started in 1989 to train community leaders. Leader Training for Parent Workshops, part of HSI's New Partnerships program, are based on the premise that interested community groups can become a powerful force in increasing parent involvement in schools. The workshops typically last two days. The materials include management training guides, grade-specific learning activities, relevant research, and reproducible home learning activities.

Several spinoffs have emerged from the first MegaSkills training efforts. A recent program targeted at teachers is called MegaSkills Essentials for the Classroom. The MegaSkills Kids Initiative, introduced in 1992, targets children directly. Most recently, a MegaSkills Hispanic Initiative has been implemented.

The 10 MegaSkills
Confidence: feeling able to do it.
Motivation: wanting to do it.
Effort: being willing to work hard.
Responsibility: doing what's right.
Initiative: moving into action.
Perseverance: completing what you start.
Caring: showing concern for others.
Teamwork: working with others.
Common Sense: using good judgment.
Problem solving: putting what you know and what you can do to action.

Quality Education Project

Initiated in California in 1982 to mobilize support for education among parents of low-income and minority students, the Quality Education Project has evolved into a highly structured school-based program. The project seeks to improve home-school communications, build family support for schools, develop parent education to encourage parent-child interaction, and encourage home learning activities to reinforce skills taught at school. The program of this nonprofit organization includes trained site coordinators, staff development, parent training, resource materials, and intensive technical assistance to school personnel.

In 1992, researchers Fruchter, Galletta, and White reported the project was addressing specific barriers to involvement, such as:

- Low-income and minority families often are geographically, culturally, and psychologically distant from schools.
- Parents face extraordinary demands on time and energy as they struggle to meet their family's needs.
- Race and class biases have traditionally shaped and limited the culture of schools.
- Teachers lack the training to work collaboratively with families.

Parents Assuring Student Success (PASS)

The PASS program evolved from three years of collaboration between parents and school administrators in Gary, Indiana. Directed by John Ban, professor of education and a member of the Gary Task Force on Street Gangs and School Discipline, PASS encourages parents to become directly involved in the education of their children. Eight activity modules address key areas in which parents can make a difference: attitude, home environment, study skills, homework, note-taking, exams, memory/thinking skills, and reading. Numerous exercises are suggested for a variety of home study situations.

The PASS program specifically targets the parents of at-risk students in urban areas. It emphasizes four strategies:
1. PASS workshops should be geared to neighborhoods.
2. Parent teams should plan PASS workshops.
3. Workshops should include social as well as learning activities.
4. Workshop recruiting should target "needy" parents and give them preferential treatment. (This strategy focuses on the fact that apathy runs high among parents of at-risk children and it is often difficult to get the parents to training sessions.)

National Parent Teacher Association

Today's parent involvement programs must be flexible and inclusive, according to the National Parent Teacher Association.

The increase in families with two working parents or with a single working parent has put new demands on a family's time, making flexibility essential to any involvement effort, explained Ja net Crouse, chair of the National PTA's education commission. Not too long ago, PTA meetings were only held during the day. Now PTA groups are trying to be more responsive to family needs, often holding meetings on weekends or during the evening. An array of other PTA-sponsored activities — lunch hours with children, "Donuts for Dads" breakfasts, or family spaghetti dinners with student entertainment — also recognize the needs of today's families.

In addition to visiting schools and other active types of involvement, Crouse pointed out some of the "invisible" ways parents can get involved: pledging to get their children to school on time each day, reading to a child in the home, or turning off the television for three hours each afternoon. Educators need to let parents know they appreciate this behind-the-scenes-support, she said.

Extended family. To reflect the changing demographics of America's families, the National PTA now uses the broader term parent/family involvement.

"Caregivers are not strictly parents anymore.... There may be grandparents, extended family, or foster parents raising kids," said Crouse. Parent/family includes all these different individuals and communicates the important role each plays in a child's education, she added.

The National Parent Teacher Association publishes several publications and resources for educators, ranging from legislative materials to conflict resolution techniques. A recent planning guide, *A Leaders' Guide To Managing Parent and Family Involvement*, helps local PTAs strengthen parent and community ties, built around three parent roles: (1) parents as participants in their child's education, (2) school volunteers and supporters, and (3) decision makers. The guidelines suggest activities both for parents who have not previously been involved and for parents who want to become more involved.

Chapter 4
Principles and Strategies for Implementation

What makes a "good" parent involvement program? Why do some schools seem warm and welcoming, while parents may feel threatened or unappreciated in others? Successful parent involvement programs have three common characteristics, according to a guide published by the Northwest Regional Educational Laboratory. Specifically, effective programs are:

1. **A schoolwide priority.** Programs are given adequate support, which includes written school and district policies establishing parent involvement as a legitimate and desired activity. Adequate funding ensures the program's consistency over time. The principal and other administrators provide leadership and encouragement. Staff are allocated time to coordinate activities. Space and equipment are provided, as well as food, transportation, and child care as needed for parent meetings.

2. **A community-based effort.** School personnel work in partnership with parents and other community members so that all players have a strong sense of ownership. Types of involvement and activities are planned jointly. Nothing is imposed unilaterally by the school or the community. School personnel have a good understanding of the community's history, leadership, role models, and appropriate communication channels. Activities address issues of concern to the community.

3. **Characterized by well-defined but flexible roles and responsibilities.** Training is provided to both staff and parents to help them understand these roles and responsibilities and to learn ways to collaborate more effectively. Mechanisms are in place to facilitate open, two-way communication among the various key players. Administrators, teachers, outreach workers, parents, other community members, and children — each group has some knowledge of the values and expectations of the other groups and of appropriate ways to communicate across groups. Players accept and respect diverse viewpoints.

Personal outreach to all parents is intensive and ongoing. Specially trained staff use a variety of media and activities to engage families and other community members in a wide variety of culturally appropriate involvement opportunities. All players continuously evaluate and revise activities.

What Do Successful Programs Have in Common?

Based on experience with parents, teachers, and administrators, and an analysis of research and program efforts, education writer Rhoda McShane Becher outlined a set of principles that characterize successful parent involvement programs. The principles fall into two categories: (1) her perspectives about parents and (2) her research and experience on program implementation.

According to Becher:

- Parents already make important contributions. Successful programs emphasize the strengths of parents and let them know that these strengths are valued.
- Parents can make additional contributions. Successful programs help parents identify new things they are capable of doing.
- Parents can learn new parenting techniques. This perspective does not imply a criticism of existing parental practices. It suggests that parents have both the ability and interest to expand their parenting strategies and techniques.
- Parents have important perspectives on their children. Successful programs recognize that these parental perspectives are useful to teachers.
- Parent-child relationships are different from teacher-child relationships. Successful programs recognize and use these differences. The activities suggested for parents to use with their children at home make use of family situations in reaching goals and incorporate consultation with parents in selecting and developing home activities.
- Parents' perspectives about involvement are important.

In successful parent involvement programs, the process, efforts, and activities are viewed from the perspective of the parents rather than from that of the staff.

- Most parents really care about their children and successful parent involvement programs hold and express this belief.
- Parents have many reasons for involvement. Successful programs make clear the purposes of parent participation and the ways parents might best work with their children.

Becher's principles related to successful program implementation are:

- Goals, purposes, and activities are matched.
- Staff skills and available resources are considered. Successful programs look at the staff's development and try to do what is reasonable and productive rather than trying to "do it all."
- Variations in parents' skills are recognized. Successful programs reflect the idea that there are many ways for parents to be involved and that all parents do not need to be involved in the same ways.
- Program activities are flexible and creative so they can be appropriate for, and responsive to, particular needs.
- Expectations, roles, and responsibilities are communicated. Successful parent involvement programs have clear task expectations, roles, and responsibilities, all of which are communicated to parents.
- Parents are involved in decision making, and administrative decisions are explained with a strong emphasis on communicating information.
- Problems are expected, but solutions are emphasized. Policies and procedures for dealing with problems are developed and communicated to parents.
- Optimum, not maximum, involvement is sought so that all those involved enjoy rather than resent their involvement.

Good news is welcome. Carole Ames, M. Khoju, and T. Watkins, researchers for the Appalachia Educational Laboratory, examined the relationship between school-to-home communication and parents' perceptions and beliefs. They found that parents who receive frequent and positive messages from teachers tend to get more involved in their children's education than parents who do not receive such communications. Negative communication "may only discourage parents and help them feel less comfortable with the school and their role as helper," they found. Consequently, researchers suggest that teachers avoid focusing on children's deficiencies and instead tell parents about their child's progress.

No cookie-cutter approach

Researchers Anne Henderson, Carl Marburger, and Theodora Ooms indicate that because schools differ from one another, there is "no one set of practices or characteristics, to which we can point and say, 'Aha! That is the definitive partnership school.'" They believe, however, schools must adopt some fundamental principles if they don't want their attempts at parent involvement to fall short.

In a partnership school, the principal and other school administrators actively express and promote the philosophy of partnership with all families and the community at large. Every aspect of the school climate is open, helpful, and friendly, and communication with parents is frequent, clear, and two-way. The school recognizes its responsibility to forge a partnership with all families in the school, not simply with those most easily available. This includes working parents, divorced parents without custody of their children, minority families, and families who don't speak English. Parents are treated as collaborators in the educational process and are encouraged, both formally and informally, to comment on school policies and, on some issues, to share in the decision making.

In *Strategies for Increasing the Involvement of Underrepresented Families in Education*, Susan Freedman,

Barbara Ascheim, and Ross Zerchykov of the Massachusetts Department of Education suggest that schools may have to make extraordinary efforts in order to involve these families:

> Schools must be willing to experiment with new approaches to home-school interaction; schools must be willing to restructure in ways that address families' needs for flexible time frames, child care, and transportation. Schools may need to adopt an expanded definition of their mission and collaborate with other community service providers in providing educational services to parents whose life circumstances prevent them from being as involved as they may want to be in their children's schooling....It is important to reach out to parents. If some parents are not going into the school, the school may need to go to where the parents are and provide them with incentives and the support to become involved.

IMPLEMENTATION STRATEGIES

Research from the Committee for Citizens in Education and others indicates that successful parent involvement programs are developed and implemented similarly and have like characteristics:

- The school coordinates activities at least half the time.
- School and community assess together their needs and resources.
- There is common understanding of the roles parents and staff will play.
- Parents are actively recruited and are selected and assigned carefully.
- Training is provided for parents and staff.
- Multiple communication channels are established and maintained.
- Continuing support services are provided for parent activities.
- Frequent opportunities are provided for evaluation and feedback.

Fort Lee School District

The principles and strategies identified by researchers for a successful parent and community involvement effort are reflected in the Fort Lee, New Jersey, School District's parent involvement program. The district occupies some 2½ square miles at the foot of the George Washington Bridge — the world's busiest — about 5,000 feet from New York City, near one of the largest drug dealing centers on the East Coast. The majority of Fort Lee's 30,000 residents work in Manhattan. The district's 3,000-plus students are 50 percent Caucasian, 42 percent Asian, 6 percent Hispanic, and 2 percent other racial and ethnic groups.

According to Superintendent Alan Sugarman, Fort Lee is really not a community, demographically or socioeconomically:

> If powerlessness is the scourge of our contemporary society, the students at Fort Lee High School would in fact epitomize this status, particularly if the school — the central agency in Fort Lee on behalf of youth — did not organize programs of community interaction.

The major components of Fort Lee's effort are described below.

- **Parent involvement committee.** Approximately 40 parents meet with the district's administrative council regularly to work out ways to increase and improve parent participation and involvement. These recommendations have been incorporated into school district operations:
  — A newsletter, which deals with student and family learning concerns, is sent home from each school.
  — The personal touch has become a watchword. Principals and teachers contact parents by telephone to commend and recommend.
  — A resource file has been developed in each school so that parents may be tapped to give presentations to small and large groups.
  — Principals suggest to PTA presidents the efficacy of inviting certain teacher specialists to meetings.
  — Principals have established curriculum committees composed of administrators, parents, teachers, and

students to discuss subject areas, concerns, and management directions.
— Parent instructional resource centers consisting of books and other materials have been incorporated into media centers, and parents have been notified of the availability of these resources.
— A "Principal Caught Me Reading" program has been instituted in every elementary and middle school.
— Corps of parents have been enlisted in every school to help orient new parents.
— More programs are held in the evening so that more parents can attend.
— Assignment brochures have been developed so that parents, students, and teachers participate equally in determining classroom assignments and their completion.
— Parent-student advisory councils at each school are helping to facilitate on-site management in the district.

- **School and Community Service Program.** Fort Lee's School and Community Service Program has received state and national recognition. It is a community-based learning experience that permits high school students to volunteer their time to help those in need. Students may choose their own assignments from many service options in education, social services, health, and community welfare. They might work as tutors in elementary school or as aides in a senior citizen center, or they might help care for the sick and handicapped in local hospitals.

  Administrators point out that, while credit is given upon the completion of 50 hours in the program, this credit serves only to legitimize the importance of service in the general program and curriculum at Fort Lee High School.

- **Mentorship Program.** This program provides an opportunity for high school students to gain on-site career experience and to become involved with carefully selected professionals in the community. The value of this opportunity to associate with positive role models cannot be overestimated. Through this experience, students discover firsthand the subtleties of a career, become better equipped to make intelligent decisions, and may be able to identify with someone who has "made it." More important, the mentorship enhances the educational process by removing the wall between classroom learning and real-world experience.

- **Asian Integration Committee.** For two years, a committee has studied the impediments to effective integration of the Asian and non-Asian communities in Fort Lee. A list of constraints was identified, and attempts are being made to address them. For example, a cadre of non-Asian parents regularly tutor Asian adults in each other's homes, which has helped these parents from diverse backgrounds bond with each other.
- **Unilever Liaison.** Unilever International, a worldwide industrial conglomerate, has adopted the Fort Lee School District, Fort Lee High School, and the Fort Lee science program.

High school science students can become involved in hands-on activities in the Unilever plant. In addition:

— Scientists serve as mentors in the high school science program and tutor science students.
— The company presents assemblies and provides career education programs, particularly for high school students interested in a science career.
— Company personnel provide consultation and assistance to staff and administration in environmental education, leadership in science-oriented field trips, orientation and assistance in better understanding of science equipment, and consultation with staff in the development of science fairs.
— Unilever employs selected school staff members during the summer.

- **Municipal Alliance Committee.** The 40-member Municipal Alliance Committee, composed of school and non-school personnel, has worked together to develop a number of drug abuse prevention programs. In 1993, Fort Lee was one of seven high schools in New Jersey nominated for the U.S.

Office of Education's Drug-Free Recognition Program.
- **Community Crisis Response Team.** Fort Lee School District has developed a state-acclaimed model for crisis management involving community members, school personnel, police and fire department officials, and others who meet regularly to train participants in how to deal with potential crises. Each school has developed scenarios for dealing with crises such as a murder-suicide in the high school, a plane crashing into an elementary school, and food poisoning at the middle school. In drills lasting half a day, parents, teachers, administrators, agency representatives, and students work on developing effective ways to respond.

For more information, contact Alan W. Sugarman, superintendent, Fort Lee School District, 255 Whiteman St., Fort Lee, NJ 07024; (201) 585-4600.

Culpeper County Public Schools

"No matter how hospitable the setting is made to get parents to school and involved, very few actually do make a consistent commitment," says Paul Asciolla, a program director with the Culpeper County, Virginia, Public Schools. "If parents don't come to you, then you have to go to the parents."

Among working parents, time is often the biggest barrier to school involvement. To overcome this time bind, the Culpeper schools have worked with local employers to provide parent education in the workplace.

Through an alliance with the local Chamber of Commerce, businesses willing to participate in a workplace parent education program were polled. Merillat Corporation, a manufacturer of kitchen cabinets, agreed to be the first site.

The program relies on a three-way contribution from business, the school district, and parents. Culpeper schools conduct free, one-hour parenting courses in the Merillat cafeteria for five weeks. Merillat gives employees a half-hour of paid release time at the end of a shift to attend the classes, and employees donate another half-hour of their own time.

More than 65 employees have taken the classes, on topics

ranging from children's developmental stages to discipline and how to say "No" to illegal substances without losing friends. Classes were offered for parents of children in grades K-6 and parents of middle and high school students. Asciolla worked with Merillat management and employees to design the curriculum and select the instructors, who were teachers, counselors, and parents that participated in train-the-trainer sessions.

The Culpeper model was reviewed by the Shenandoah Valley Alliance for Education. A similar program was launched at Virginia Metalcrafters in Waynesboro, Virginia, and several other worksites in the surrounding Shenandoah Valley have expressed interest.

For more information, contact Paul Asciolla, drug education and community information specialist, Culpeper County Public Schools, 1051 N. Main St. Extended, Culpeper, VA 22701; (703) 825-3677.

Dunbar Public Schools

Students from three Dunbar, West Virginia, elementary schools — two are Chapter 1 schools — board a van twice a week when their school day is over. The van takes them to a local community church where the students have an hour of math enrichment and tutoring in a program called Saving Our Children.

Now in its second year, the program was organized by Pat Kusimo, director of the Appalachia Educational Laboratory's education services program. The Rev. James Patterson, pastor of the church housing the program, explains, "We wanted a program in which members of the community could mobilize themselves and have a positive impact on their children's education, as well as on other social problems that are prevalent within our community." The program planners recruited parent and community volunteers, and involved local high school students and preservice teachers from a nearby college as tutors.

The program is not limited to at-risk students, although teachers are asked to identify children who are at risk of failing math or who are at risk because of their behavior. Once potential enrollees are identified, volunteers send letters home or make home visits to explain the program and to obtain permission for the children to participate. Student participation is strictly voluntary.

Kusimo believes the real value of an enrichment program is that it sparks children's interest in a particular subject. Students discover that math is more than paperwork, and they find they can learn math while having a lot of fun.

Although no formal evaluation data have been gathered, Kusimo notes that some children who were failing math pulled their grades up to C's by the end of the school year. One school principal noticed a definite improvement in her students' academic achievement in math. Kusimo says, "To me, the best sign of success is that enrollment has gone up and the kids attend on a regular basis." Program enrollment doubled in the second year, with a high turnout of students and their parents at a year-end banquet.

For more information, contact Pat Kusimo, director, educational services, Appalachia Educational Laboratory, P.O. Box 1348, Charleston, WV 25325; (304)347-0400.

Eastwood Elementary School

Eastwood Elementary School is part of the Big Rapids, Michigan, Public School System. Eastwood's Affective Intervention Model (AIM) consists of 10 component programs "in which members work together to 'Create the Future' through a collaborative project designed to increase learning, strengthen families, improve the quality of life in neighborhoods, develop leadership, and promote involvement in the challenges of creating one society that values children as its greatest resource."

AIM is composed of:
- **Home-School Coordinator.** Through a series of "kitchen conversations", the coordinator helps parents

develop plans to reach their own hopes, dreams, and aspirations for themselves and their children. These plans are included in a home-school planning process. Family support includes parent advocacy, student assistance activities, and networking with many community groups.

- **Home-School Learning Teams.** Each classroom program is conducted by an instructional team of a teacher and aide. Every job description at Eastwood was re-created to provide family-oriented learning support in the life of each child. Chapter 1 and other special needs students receive extra help from staff whose roles include two hours of Chapter 1 and two hours of regular instruction.
- **Soaring Eagles.** Thirty-two students and five staff members spend 10 mornings together in mid-August in a nonacademic setting. They focus on improving math and reading skills to get ready for the beginning of school. Serving as the culminating activity of a summer family activities plan, the program teaches students school success skills, including listening, cooperative learning, following directions, and respect for others.
- **The Community Coalition.** The coalition began with an award-winning school-business partnership formed in 1991 between Eastwood and the Michigan Consolidated Gas Company. It now has expanded to include a wide variety of partners. Most partners participate in at least two or three of the program components and choose to be part of the Eastwood School Improvement/Grant Steering Committee.
- **Neighborhood Learning Centers.** These centers were initiated by Eastwood and the Big Rapids Housing Commission Resident Council to provide a supportive place for families to assist in their children's learning. They are operated four days a week for 1 1/2 hours by volunteer tutors and paid adults. At the centers, fami-

lies and students can learn, explore culture, participate in recreation, experience positive role models, relate to peer mentors, and build their community.

- **Child Watch.** This is a communitywide safe child program initiated locally on the east side of Big Rapids in partnership with the local law enforcement agency, MichCon, and the Housing Commission Resident Council. The project was initiated as a cultural mainstream learning opportunity and a family esteem-raising effort.

- **Family Resource Center.** The Mid-Michigan Alliance for Community Development established the neighborhood Family Resource Center-Story Book Child Care in early 1992, with some assistance from Eastwood. The director is jointly funded to make parent education, child care, support groups, crisis child care, family resources, and respite child care more available for coalition programs.

- **Cooperative Family Camp.** When this book was published, three overnight cooperative camping sessions were being planned to strengthen family relationships and build a sense of community. The idea was that families would live in cabins and share in work, recreation, and learning activities over a three-day period. Sessions were planned to include parenting, water safety, family games, group programs, and environmental understanding.

- **Planning-Evaluation.** A variety of methods is used to provide all levels of the partnership with quality planning, evaluation, and case conference time, including biweekly teachers' and/or aides' meetings, classroom team release time, steering committee meetings, team interviews, Community Coalition partners' meetings, annual school meetings, individual classroom open house orientations, and parent and staff surveys. The research design is implemented each year in cooperation with the Ferris State University Social Work Program.

- **Sharing-Networking.** In addition to membership in the 84-member League of Schools Reaching Out, the Community Coalition maintains its own home-school-community information network with a growing number of other schools and agencies around the country. Presentations are available for conferences, and workshops can be developed on request. Visitations and training are available on site. An electronic network is under development.

For more information, contact David Borth, principal, or Sherry Franklin, home/school coordinator, Eastwood Elementary School, 410 N. Third St., Big Rapids, MI 49307; (616) 796-5556.

SETTING THE TONE THROUGH LEADERSHIP

School principals and classroom teachers play critical roles in organizing, developing, and implementing effective parent involvement programs. In *Schools and Communities Together: A Guide to Parent Involvement,* Karen Reed Wikelund, researcher and writer for the Northwest Regional Educational Laboratory, states that the "principal's leadership sets the tone — the climate — of the school....The principal must provide the overall school leadership to establish and maintain the parent involvement program, including visible moral and financial support and required staff participation."

Joyce Epstein of Johns Hopkins University says that the role of administrators can be described as "coordinating, managing, supporting, funding, and recognizing parent involvement." Administrative functions within these categories include disseminating research findings, sponsoring staff meetings and inservice workshops, documenting existing efforts throughout the school, encouraging teamwork among teachers to develop activities for parents and to share results, providing incentives for teachers to create parent involvement activities, recognizing the efforts of both parents and teachers, and developing a positive attitude that encourages long-term development of parent involvement activities.

Teachers are a pivotal link

Without committed teachers, schools will have great difficulty involving parents in the simplest activities.

The degree that teachers believe that such involvement can be a positive factor in academic achievement greatly affects the success of parental involvement programs.

Epstein and her colleague Henry Becker have identified several key elements in teachers' behavior that influence their willingness to engage in parent involvement efforts.

Their research shows that:
- Teachers who use a variety of methods to involve parents believe it is possible to involve all parents regardless of their income and educational levels.
- Teachers who have had previous positive contact with the family are more likely to support and use parent involvement activities.
- Teachers have more positive attitudes about parent involvement when principals and other colleagues also support this concept.

Teachers' concerns. It is important to realize that while teachers may value parental involvement, they don't always know where to begin. As Epstein observed in 1982 :

> While teachers think that more parent involvement would help to improve student achievement, they report that they don't know how to initiate or accomplish such a program and have reservations about whether or not teachers could motivate parents (who would not normally do so) to take the time to provide informal learning opportunities at home.

In 1984, Rhoda McShane Becher identified teacher attitudes that can impede parent involvement activities. In reviewing research studies, she found that teachers were concerned about how to (1) involve parents and at the same time maintain their expert role, (2) balance consideration for the group with consideration for the individual child, and (3) find the time necessary to plan parent involvement.

Teachers also were concerned that parents might try to take over teaching responsibilities and not follow the teacher's instructions and the school's regulations; that parents might disrupt the classroom because they didn't know how to work with children; and that parents might not keep their commitments and might breach confidentiality.

How Can Teachers Successfully Involve Parents?

- Maintain high expectations for every child to learn and achieve.
- Examine their own assumptions about ability and interest (regarding behavior, nonstandard English or lack of English, physical appearance, or family background) and remain alert to negative images.
- Take time to get to know the community (or communities) represented by the children they teach — the history of their interactions with the school, their values and customs, local heroes, favorite pastimes, child-rearing practices, worries, and aspirations.
- Treat all children and their families with respect.
- Welcome every family into their classroom and make them feel comfortable in the school.
- Establish and maintain open, two-way communication with parents and other family members.
- Provide a variety of options for parents to collaborate with them in teaching children (including homework activities, class projects, volunteer work in the classroom and on field trips, fundraising).
- Participate in staff training about parent involvement.
- Participate in school activities designed to help staff and families get to know each other.
- View cultural diversity as a resource and teach children to value it.
- Identify and use ways to validate children's experiences outside of school and incorporate them into instructional activities.
- Collaborate with other professionals and parents to address particular children's learning or emotional problems.
- Take stock of their parent involvement activities regularly with input from other key players, and revise them as necessary.
- Never give up on any child.

Source: Karen Reed Wikelund. *Schools and Communities Together: A Guide to Parent Involvement*, 1990.

INSERVICE TRAINING

Most administrators and teachers have not had preservice training in parent involvement, so inservice training is necessary for involvement efforts to become an integral part of any school or system. Researchers David Williams and Nancy Feyl Chavkin state that an ideal training program has three essential components: 1) an understanding of the personal framework of the teacher, 2) an understanding of the effective models of parent involvement, and 3) development of a conceptual framework based on theoretical and research material concerning the developmental nature of parent involvement in schools.

In 1993, the U.S. Department of Education's Oliver Moles and Diane D'Angelo suggested that school staff should receive training in:

- Greeting and meeting parents and creating an inviting and nonthreatening climate.
- Reaching out and not sitting together as the 'school choir' at PTA meetings.
- Telephoning parents and using positive language.
- Learning about and understanding cultural/racial/ethnic groups that are different from their own groups (and even sometimes learning about their own groups!).
- Using volunteers effectively.
- Understanding why it is painful for some families to get involved.
- Seeking parent representatives for the school parent management team.
- Planning activities that do not involve parents and teachers in too many evening meetings.

Support for Teachers

Administrators and others can help teachers develop and improve their parent involvement efforts in the following ways:

- Help teachers realize they already possess a number of the skills necessary for establishing successful programs.
- Support their efforts, particularly when these efforts don't work as planned.
- Help teachers identify their feelings about various aspects of parent involvement.
- Help them develop conflict resolution rather than conflict avoidance strategies.
- Help change teacher perspectives about parent involvement so they begin to see the process from the perspective of the parents rather than solely from their own viewpoint.
- Help select parent involvement activities that meet the goals and purposes of the program rather than because they look interesting or useful.
- Remind teachers to tap the same skills they use in making friends when they're reaching out to parents.

Source: Becher, Rhoda McShane. *Parent Involvement: A Review of Research and Principles of Successful Practice*, 1984.

DEALING WITH PRESSURE GROUPS

Administrators, teachers, and other school personnel often find themselves faced with individuals and groups outside the school that may attempt to apply pressure on the schools to bring about some type of change. In these conflict situations, school administrators, particularly principals, often find themselves serving as mediators. An administrator can then either choose to impose his or her will on the parties involved or to see the situation as an opportunity to improve existing conditions, as writers Howard Margolis and Kenneth Tewel stated in 1988:

Well-managed conflict helps develop creative, synergistic solutions to undesirable situations and a broadened understanding of the nature of the real problems facing people. Well-managed conflict also improves interpersonal relationships and stimulates healthy interaction, interest, and involvement in the real problem and its solutions. It also increases commitment to agreed-upon solutions and heightens feelings of competence and satisfaction.

Types of community interest groups

In 1984, John Harrigan, a professor at Hamlin University in Minnesota, identified four broad categories of interest groups that may pressure schools in order to bring about some type of change:

- Economically motivated groups attempt to influence how much money is spent.
- Professionally motivated groups primarily provide service to their members.
- Public agency groups provide public officials a chance to exchange ideas, lobby collectively, and get information on how their agency might be affected by proposed policy.
- Ideological groups claim to represent a public interest and usually arise in response to a specific issue.

Seek common ground. The administrator, whether as the facilitator or as a party to the conflict, might try a well-tested problem-solving approach to resolving the situation. Key to the success of such an approach is trust building and active listening. The American Association of School Administrators provides several tips for dealing with pressure groups:

- Be open and honest. Be a good listener. Hide nothing.
- Be sure that everyone who needs to know is informed of your contacts with representatives of the pressure group.
- Get together for a visit with an individual or a small group. Try to clear the air and get rid of myths.
- Keep in mind that often members of a group only

want to be sure their voices are heard.
- Seek a common denominator if possible.
- Be adaptable if adaptability is reasonable.
- Apply negotiation techniques. Communicate well and strive for consensus.

Chapter 5
Policy Statements: Making it Official

School leaders' best intentions of involving parents may not go far unless they institutionalize plans and practices through effective policies. These should encompass school boards as well as staff, and be both comprehensive and specific.

Enlisting Board Support

In its 1988 publication, *First Teachers: Parental Involvement in the Public Schools*, the National School Boards Association suggests that, to have any long-term effect, parent involvement programs must grow out of a carefully planned school board policy.

To develop this policy, NSBA proposes a five-step planning process:
1. Assess current policies and needs.
2. Establish board policy and the board's commitment to that policy.
3. Communicate the policy.
4. Develop a plan to implement the policy.
5. Evaluate the policy.

The National Coalition for Parent Involvement in Education recommends that parent involvement policies should be developed with input from teachers, administrators, parents, students, and other community members. Care should be taken to recognize diverse family structures, circumstances, and responsibilities that might impede parent participation.

In 1991, Janet Chrispeels, an education writer and professor at the University of California in Santa Barbara, said school board policy should commit the board to:
- Involve parents as partners in school governance, including shared decision making and advisory functions.
- Establish effective two-way communication with all parents, respecting the diversity and differing needs

67

of families.
- Develop strategies and programs at schools to enable active participation of parents.
- Provide support and coordination for school staff and parents to implement and sustain appropriate parent involvement from kindergarten through grade 12.
- Use schools to connect students and families with community resources that provide educational enrichment and support.

What Can School Boards and Superintendents Do?

Anne Henderson, Carl Marburger, and Theodora Ooms of the National Committee for Citizens in Education suggest several actions school boards and superintendents can take together to strengthen parent involvement initiatives:

- Provide the resources needed to educate parents and teachers to use parent-teacher conferences productively.
- Hire and train community outreach workers based in all the schools to work with families who do not readily come to school or whose cultural background requires that special efforts be made to communicate with them.
- Develop a clear districtwide policy regarding the rights of noncustodial parents to be sent progress reports and other information on their child.
- Require that some portion of staff development each year be devoted to parent-teacher collaboration.
- Permit and encourage individual schools to invite community organizations to run after-school recreation programs, child care programs, and study halls for both younger and older children in the building.
- Encourage local businesses to donate resources to schools, provide release time for their employees to volunteer in school, and release time for parents to attend school functions and conferences.

continued on next page

- Develop a districtwide school calendar, daily schedule, bus schedule, and emergency policies that are sensitive to parents' realities and balance their needs with others' needs.
- Develop cooperative agreements with community service agencies to provide liaison staff to work in the schools as consultants and to facilitate referrals.

School District Policies

Frequently, school districts will spell out their parent involvement goals and activities by developing and adopting formal policies. A sampling of district policies follows.

McAllen, Texas, Independent School District

The goals of McAllen's Parent Involvement Program are:
- To provide effective and positive communications between schools, homes, and the community.
- To promote parent and community involvement so that parents and community members become effective partners in the improvement of McAllen schools.
- To provide parenting education, awareness, training programs, and activities that are beneficial for parents and their children.

The program's objectives are:
- To develop mutually beneficial partnerships between schools and community entities.
- To provide educational programs that strengthen parenting skills and help parents provide educational assistance to their children.
- To expand linkages with social, educational, health, and other human resource agencies.
- To implement special evening educational programs for parents and students.
- To meet the needs of at-risk students and their parents.
- To keep parents better informed about school and community resources.
- To increase communication between teachers and

parents regarding the academic performance and development of students.
- To develop parents' confidence and ability levels so that they can become effective leaders in school and community activities.

Baltimore, Maryland, City Public Schools

Baltimore's Community Involvement Policy states:

Rationale
In order to establish collaboration between neighborhoods and schools, the schools must develop and expand effective community involvement programs. Increased involvement in all schools by civic, business, university, church, fraternal, and parent groups will create a positive bond, a tie that will produce a stronger educational system and will improve the quality of life for the citizens of Baltimore.

Policy
The Baltimore City Public Schools system supports effective, continuing community involvement at all levels in every school. Schools will encourage this involvement, providing communication and training, decision making and collaboration, in an effort to implement the school system's goals and to realize the plans of individual schools.

Each Baltimore school is responsible for developing a plan to increase 1) parent/community involvement, 2) volunteers, and 3) partnerships.

Pomona, California, Unified School District

The district's Parent/Guardian Involvement Policy states: The superintendent or designee shall ensure opportunities for parent/guardian involvement by means that shall include an annual evaluation of the following guidelines:

1. Helping parents develop parenting skills and foster conditions at home that support their children's efforts in learning. This may be accomplished through the development of parent

training and informational brochures, workshops, and other activities for parents of compensatory education students. The topics could include health and safety, school preparation for children, and building positive home conditions that support school learning and behavior.

2. Providing parents with the knowledge of techniques to assist their children in learning at home. These techniques include reading to children and listening to children read; encouraging study habits that include a regular time and place for homework, as well as monitoring and assisting with homework as guided by teachers at each grade level; and setting standards and limits for the use of time and social interactions of the students, conversing with children about school and other topics, and exploring curricular and career choices.

3. Providing access to and coordinating community and support services for children and families. This may include locating and actively encouraging parents to use community resource programs and agencies, including senior citizen tutorial programs, business/school partnerships, city/school partnerships, college work study/help programs, and library/museum programs.

4. Promoting clear two-way communication between school and family about school programs and children's progress. This happens best when both school staff and parents freely initiate and promptly respond to communication requests. Activities to encourage this communication are frequent discussions between teachers and parents, school newsletters, back-to-school/open house activities, and weekend informational workshops/training sessions.

ADMINISTRATIVE CONSIDERATIONS

In addition to a thoughtfully developed school board policy, effective parent involvement programs require strong leadership and cooperative planning. In 1987, researchers Nancy Feyl Chavkin and David Williams conducted an extensive survey of superintendents, school board presidents, and parents in the six-state area served by the Southwest Educational Development Laboratory to find out how administrators and parents felt about parent involvement, what types of district policies existed, and what guidelines would help administrators enhance parent involvement.

The results identified two decisive needs: (1) "participation and collaboration between schools and parents in interpreting and developing common parent involvement goals" and (2) "a partnership approach" to developing and implementing the parent involvement program.

Based on their survey results, Chavkin and Williams developed a set of recommendations for superintendents and school board members who want to enhance parent involvement efforts:

- Look beyond traditional ways of working with parents.
- Collaborate with parents to develop a clear statement about the goals of parent involvement.
- Develop formal school district policies.
- Provide instruction and inservice training for teachers and administrators.
- Ask parents how they want to be involved in the education of their children.
- Make certain a variety of involvement opportunities is available.
- Ensure that parents are fully involved at all levels of the educational system.
- View various types of parent involvement as a developmental process.
- Make appropriate kinds of resources available for parent involvement efforts.

Chapter 6
Involving Hard-to-Reach and At-Risk Parents

In their values, expectations, and environment, most schools reflect middle-class families and, generally, do quite well in educating middle-class children. But how effective are school initiatives for involving at-risk and other groups of parents?

Based on her research, education writer Lynn Balster Liontos agrees that the challenge for educators is "to communicate with and involve parents who are poor, nonwhite, or speak a language other than English." This growing realization may explain why many of today's parent involvement efforts are aimed at low-income families, families from minority cultures, and families with other risk factors, such as teenage parents.

New Directions in Parent Involvement

Norm Fruchter, Anne Galletta, and J. Lynne White of the Academy for Educational Development in 1992 studied 18 parent involvement programs. In varying degrees, the programs' components represent different approaches to parent involvement, including:

- A strong commitment to involve low-income and disadvantaged parents in activities ultimately aimed at improving student academic achievement.
- Origins in universities or nonprofit institutions, with resulting sponsorship, implementation, and evaluation maintained by these external institutions.
- Significant public sector support through funding from federal grants, state legislative allocation, or district buy-in, as well as private-sector support through foundation or corporate grants.
- A strong commitment to reduce the gap between home and school cultures by shaping program components to respond to, and build on, the values, structures, and languages of home cultures.

- A strong commitment to develop program components so that parents are empowered by their participation.

Involved parents, improved learning. Parent empowerment — defined as providing the structures to help parents become active participants in shaping their children's development, learning capacity, and school experience — is a critical component of all these programs. Because most of these programs target schools and districts serving low-income and disadvantaged constituencies, it is possible that a new generation of parents, empowered by their experience of active participation in shaping their children's schools, will emerge to transform schools that need a great deal of help in serving all of our nation's children.

Reaching the Hard-To-Reach

According to the National School Public Relations Association, a key factor in communicating with hard-to-reach parents is getting out of the school buildings and into the community. NSPRA suggests a variety of nontraditional ways educators can reach parents and community members:

- Hold coffee klatches with groups of parents in their homes or in other nonthreatening settings.
- Have principals, the superintendent, and board members take two hours on one Saturday per month, on a rotating basis, to make themselves available to parents at a local site such as a supermarket.
- Have principals and staff members use the telephone to share good news with parents.
- Locate community leaders and invite them to help communicate with hard-to-reach parents.
- Offer programs to meet neighborhood needs — these may not always be school-oriented.
- Provide school representatives who are fluent in the language of ethnic groups and offer English-speaking and parenting classes for adults in locations near their homes.
- Hold parent-teacher conferences in the neighborhoods — at the churches, youth centers, anywhere parents can come together easily.

Success with Urban Families

As part of their outreach to families, urban schools often must face concentrated doses of poverty, illiteracy, low English proficiency, poor health, and other factors associated with at-risk families.

Family involvement is one component of Options for Pre-Teens (OPT), a primary prevention and youth development program that successfully reaches out to young adolescents and their families in three urban districts: the Norfolk, Virginia, Public Schools; the School District of the City of Pontiac, Michigan; and the Oakland, California, Unified School District.

OPT's comprehensive approach applies current research, wisdom, and practice to positively affect the school and life experiences of children in low-income, urban communities. The superintendent and staff of participating schools have committed themselves to making fundamental changes in the way they interact with children, their families, the community, and each other.

Recognizing the common and differing needs of all families, OPT schools offer them a menu of participation options. All the schools use traditional strategies for communicating with families, such as "Back-to-School Nights," parent/teacher meetings, and report card conferences. But several innovative strategies, often giving a new twist to time-honored activities, are the mainstay of OPT family and community involvement.

Effective OPT practices in the following areas are described below.

Parent Education/Assistance for Families
- A 12-week effective parenting course is offered.
- At morning "second cup of coffee" sessions, parents gather in a small group to discuss informally issues *they* bring to the table.
- Special "night-at-school" activities for children allow parents to attend school workshops and meetings, often with transportation provided.

- Twice-monthly workshops (held once at school and once in a community facility) focus on such issues as conferencing, how to talk with your adolescent, resolving conflicts, and discipline.
- Family Walk/Talk, a parent-run morning exercise program, gives parents an opportunity to walk as a group, get to know other parents, and talk informally about issues for themselves or their children.
- Student and family advocacy with a licensed OPT social worker who helps families solve problems, facilitates family counseling groups, and provides access to community health, mental health, and social service agencies.

School/Home Communication
- Home visits from student and family advocates serve as a link between home and school.
- *Our Legacy*, the OPT monthly family newsletter, describes upcoming school and community activities and includes information for families on ways they can help their child succeed in school.
- "Post Card Progress" sends home a positive message to all parents about their child's progress.

Involvement at School
- An OPT family room in the school building welcomes all parents and provides them with their own permanent space to work or meet.
- Parent volunteers assist in classrooms and on field trips, provide orientation for families new to the school, and "teach" classes during the OPT summer program.
- OPT families participate in "Family Fun Week" where they, along with children and school staff (including principals), engage in a week-long program of education and leisure activities, like bowling or skating nights, spaghetti dinners, and special speaker events.
- The "Have Lunch with Your Child" program invites

family members to dine in the OPT family room with their children.

Involvement in Learning Activities at Home
- The Teachers Involve Parents in Schoolwork (TIPS) program encourages parents to participate in activities that build skills and attitudes and directly help the child in school. These activities include student practice skills and teacher guidance and support on how to assist their child and monitor homework.
- Parent/child interaction is encouraged through "Family Tote Bags" filled with small, interactive educational games, books, puzzles, writing paper, pencils, and a parent sign-off sheet. The bags are taken home on Wednesday each week and returned to school the following Monday.

Involvement in Governance, Decision Making, and Advocacy
- Aside from leadership in the PTA and participation on school site councils, parent communication, negotiation, and leadership skills are honed through a family involvement workshop series.
- Parents, staff, students, and community agency representatives actively participate in a school climate enhancement effort, which engages them in an intensive examination of their school; helps them formulate goals and objectives for making it a better place to learn, work, and visit; and guides them through the process of operationalizing their plans.
- Through *Our Legacy*, families are provided with information necessary to support school improvement efforts.

Community Exchange and Collaboration
- Community agencies serve as "employers" for OPT service learning activities, which foster responsibility

and caring and provide students with the opportunity for hands-on experience with community problems and the world of work.
- Neighborhood adults and representatives from local agencies are sought to participate fully in OPT school climate enhancement efforts. Local business and community leaders often speak at family involvement workshops.

The OPT program has been in full operation since 1991. A nine-year evaluation study set for the year 2000 is planned to determine the success of the program through the measurement of educational, health, and social outcomes for participating students.

OPT is sponsored by the American Association of School Administrators and is funded by the U.S. Maternal and Child Health Bureau and the following foundations: W.K. Kellogg, Robert Wood Johnson, Charles Stewart Mott, the Pew Charitable Trusts, the Kaiser Family, Stuart, S.H. Cowell, and Joseph Drown.

For more information on OPT family involvement or the program's other components, contact Sharon Adams-Taylor, director, Options for Pre-Teens, American Association of School Administrators, 1801 N. Moore St., Arlington, VA 22209-9988

When You Can't "Phone Home"

Sometimes, reaching parents is not as simple as picking up the telephone — because not all households are equipped with phones.

Using 1990 census data, William P. O'Hare of the Annie E. Casey Foundation reported the following statistics.

Though these data are for children under age six, it follows that similar conditions exist for children of all ages.

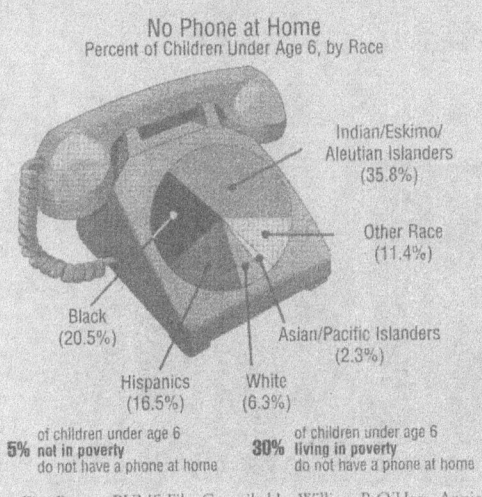

No Phone at Home
Percent of Children Under Age 6, by Race

Indian/Eskimo/Aleutian Islanders (35.8%)
Other Race (11.4%)
Black (20.5%)
Asian/Pacific Islanders (2.3%)
Hispanics (16.5%)
White (6.3%)

5% of children under age 6 not in poverty do not have a phone at home
30% of children under age 6 living in poverty do not have a phone at home

Source: 1990 Census, One-Percent PUMS File. Compiled by William P. O'Hare, Annie E. Casey Foundation

KEEPING PARENTS OF OLDER STUDENTS INVOLVED

Parent involvement is important in all phases of a child's education, from the first day of kindergarten to high school graduation. Unfortunately, studies show that parent involvement tends to taper off as children enter middle and high school, making all parents potentially hard-to-reach. Even if parents were heavily involved when their children were in elementary school, sustaining that involvement through students' teenage years can be difficult.

A 1994 study, *Running in Place*, from the research organization Child Trends reports that moderate to high parent involvement dropped from approximately 75 percent during the early elementary years to approximately 50 percent during high school. Moderately to highly involved parents were defined as those who had participated in two to three school activities, such as general or PTA meetings, sporting events, plays, and volunteer activities.

Involvement Decreases Over Time

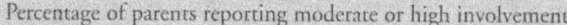

The percentage of parents who report moderate or high involvement in school activities declines as children get older.

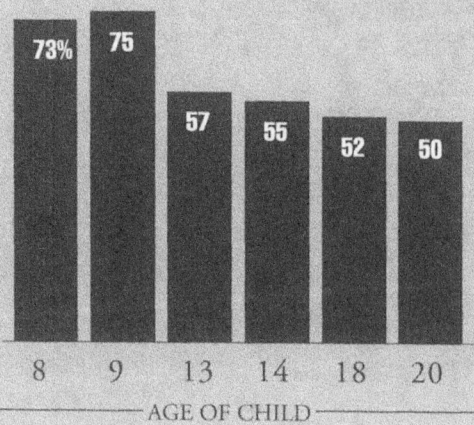

Percentage of parents reporting moderate or high involvement

73% | 75 | 57 | 55 | 52 | 50
8 | 9 | 13 | 14 | 18 | 20
AGE OF CHILD

Source: U.S. Department of Education, National Household Education Survey

The report cites lack of motivation and an unwelcome school environment as some of the reasons for parents' declining involvement. However, the authors also said "parents may be yielding too much influence to their children's friends and to other forces."

To keep the parents of older students involved, the report recommends providing school-family activities of interest to all students, including those who are not college-bound. Schools also need to let parents know that their involvement is still valuable through personal contacts, letters and other written communications, and opportunities to serve on parent advisory boards or other groups.

For example, a suburban high school in Northern Virginia invited several parents of incoming freshmen to serve on a special advisory group. Once a month, the group met with the principal to discuss informally any topics they chose, and the principal used the meetings to inform parents of important school news. Parents could serve on the board for the four years of their child's high school career.

CONCLUSION

The evidence is indisputable. Research and practice clearly show the benefits of involving parents in their children's education. As Thomas Kellaghan, director of the Educational Research Centre at St. Patrick's College in Dublin, Ireland, pointed out, "The home environment is a powerful factor in determining the academic success of students — their level of school achievement, their interest in school learning, and the number of years of schooling they will receive."

Although documentation of the benefits of parent involvement has existed for a number of years, interest in parent involvement initiatives has intensified only recently. Today, a parent and community involvement component is part of almost every educational reform initiative.

Don Davies, director of the Institute for Responsive Education, suggests several reasons for this growing interest:

- **Competitiveness:** Policymakers, economists, and corporate leaders are deeply concerned about the country's ability to remain economically competitive....Now more people realize that if the schools are to become more productive and produce more students who are able to contribute to the closing of the competitiveness gap, they will need help from parents and the community.
- **Social inequality and instability:** Many policymakers, social analysts, economists, and corporate leaders are concerned about the development of a two-tiered society of haves and have nots, with a large number of people consigned to a seemingly perpetual underclass. The failure of public schools to serve the urban and rural poor adequately is viewed as one important part of a deteriorating situation in which crime, violence, drugs, and health crises are a threat to social stability, as well as to the nation's aspiration to be just and equitable. Moreover, the threat of social inequality and

instability is closely linked with the issue of competitiveness.
- **Political reality:** The growing consensus about the importance of parents in the education and development of their children feeds on itself, and the idea has become entrenched in public opinion....[The idea is] then reflected in the expressions of public opinion and "leader opinion," which in turn influence elected policymakers. School officials and organizations read the same polls...[and] by and large they respond to the political reality.

A major issue facing American education

In their 1993 research studies, Kellaghan and others show that when home and school synchronize their emphasis on motivation and learning with children, it sets up a three-way mutually beneficial relationship. The research also shows that the socioeconomic level or cultural background of a home is less important in determining how well a child achieves than what parents contribute toward learning. As an added benefit, parent involvement also strengthens family togetherness and promotes greater community awareness.

Most importantly, when schools and parents cooperate, it sends a powerful, lifelong message to students: Learning is valuable and so are they. Schools and parents are working together to ensure students receive a high quality education that will prepare them for life's many challenges.

BIBLIOGRAPHY

Alabama Department of Education (no date). *A Plan for Excellence: Alabama's Public Schools Parental Involvement Plan.* Montgomery, AL.

America 2000, An Educational Strategy (1991). Washington, DC: U.S. Government Printing Office.

Ames, C., Khoju, M., and Watkins, T. (1994). "Teachers Should Communicate with Parents Often and Convey Positive, Encouraging Messages," *The Link*, (13)1 (Spring).

Appalachia Educational Laboratory (1994). "Math Enrichment Program Gets Parents and Community Involved," *The Link*, (13)1 (Spring).

Ban, J. R. (1993). *Parents Assuring Student Success (PASS): Achievement Made Easy by Learning Together.* Bloomington, IN: National Educational Service.

Barton, P., and Coley, R. (1992) *America's Smallest School: The Family.* Princeton, NJ: Policy Information Center, Educational Testing Service.

Becher, R. (1984). *Parent Involvement: A Review of Research and Principles of Successful Practice.* Washington, DC: National Institute of Education (ED 247 032).

Becher, R. (1984). Cited in *The Evidence Continues To Grow*, A. Henderson, ed. Washington, DC: National Committee for Citizens in Education.

Beria, N., Garlington, J., and Henderson, A. (1993). *Taking Stock: The Inventory of Family, Community, and School Support for Student Achievement.* Washington, DC: National Committee for Citizens in Education.

Boo, M. R., and Decker, L. E. (1985). *The Learning Community.* Alexandria, VA: National Community Education Association.

Burns, R. C. (1993). *Parents and Schools: From Visitors to Partners.* Washington, DC: National Education Association.

Chavkin, N. F., ed. (1993). *Families and Schools in a Pluralistic Society.* Albany, NY: State University of New York Press.

Chavkin, N. and Williams, D. (1987). "Enhancing Parent Involvement, Guidelines for Access to Important Resources for School Administrators." *Education and Urban Society,* (19)2.

Chavkin, N. F., and Williams, D. L., Jr. (1985). *Parent Involvement in Education Project.* Austin, TX: Southwest Educational Development Lab, ED 266 872.

Children's Defense Fund (1992). *The State of Children in Rural America.* Washington, DC.

Children's Defense Fund (1991). *The State of America's Children.* Washington, DC.

Chrispeels, J. (1991). "District Leadership in Parent Involvement," *Phi Delta Kappan,* (January).

Cochran, M. (1987). "The Parental Empowerment Process: Building on Family Strengths," *Equity and Choice* 4(1).

Coleman, J. S. (1991). *Policy Perspectives: Parental Involvement in Education.* Washington, DC: Office of Educational Research and Improvement, U.S. Department of Education.

Council of Chief State School Officers and National Coalition for Parent Involvement in Education (1992). *Guide to Parent Involvement Resources.* Washington, DC.

Davies, D. (1988) *Helping Parents Help Their Kids.* Washington, DC: National School Public Relations Association.

Davies, D. (1991). "Schools Reaching Out: Family, School, and Community Partnerships for Student Success," *Phi Delta Kappan.*(72) 376-80 (January).

Decker, L. (1994) *Home-School-Community Relations Trainers Manual and Study Guide.* Charlottesville, VA: Mid-Atlantic Center for Community Education.

Decker, L. (1992). "Building Learning Communities: The Realities of Educational Restructuring," *Community Education Journal,* XIX(3).

Elam, S., Rose, L., and Gallup, A. (1993). *The 25th Annual Phi Delta Kappa/Gallup Poll of the Public's Attitude Toward the Public Schools.* Princeton, NJ: Gallup Organization.

Epstein, J. (1993). "Effects on Parents of Teacher Practices of Parent Involvement," *Johns Hopkins University Report* 346, (October).

Epstein, J. (1992). *School and Family Partnerships. Report No. 6.* Baltimore, MD: The Johns Hopkins University Center on Families, Communities, Schools, and Children's Learning.

Epstein, J. (1992). "School and Family Partnerships," in M. Alkin, ed., *Encyclopedia of Educational Research, 6th Edition.* New York: MacMillan.

Epstein, J. (1987). "Parent Involvement, What Research Says to Administrators." *Education and Urban Society,* (19)2.

Epstein, J., and Becker, J. (1992). "A Survey of Teacher Practices," *Elementary School Journal.*(83)3, (November).

Epstein, J. and Herrick, S. (1990). *Implementing School and Family Partnerships in the Middle Grades: Three Evaluations of Summer Home Learning Packets, School Newsletters, and Orientation Days.* (CDS Report No. 20.) Baltimore, MD: Johns Hopkins University Center for Research on Effective Schooling for Disadvantaged Students.

Epstein, J., and Salinas, K. C. (1993). *School and Family Partnerships: Surveys and Summaries.* Baltimore, MD: Johns Hopkins University Center on Families, Communities, Schools, and Children's Learning.

Epstein, J. and Salinas, K. (1992). *Manual for Teachers: Teachers Involve Parents in Schoolwork (TIPS).* Baltimore, MD: The John Hopkins University Center on Families, Communities, Schools, and Children's Learning.

Family/School/Community Partnership, Executive Summary (no date). Tallahassee, FL: Economics Unit, Division of Vocational, Adult and Community Education, Florida Department of Education.

Flaxman, E., and Inger, M. (1991). "Parents and Schooling in the 1990s," *The ERIC Review.* (1)3 (September).

Freedman, S., Aschheim, B.,and Zerchykov, R. (1989). *Strategies for Increasing the Involvement of Underrepresented Families in Education.* Quincy, MA: Massachusetts Department of Education.

Fruchter, N., Galletta, A., and White, J. L. (1992). *New Directions in Parent Involvement.* Washington, DC: Academy for Educational Development, Inc.

Gilliam, R. (1977). "The Effects of Parent Involvement on School Achievement in Three Michigan Performance Contracting Programs." Paper presented at American Educational Research Association, New York City. (Ed 144 077).

Gregg, S. (1993). "Partnerships: Sharing Responsibility for Children," *The Link.* (Fall) Charleston, WV: Appalachia Educational Laboratory, Inc.

Hamilton, D. and Osborne, S. (1991). *Barriers to Parent Involvement in Public Schools.* Unpublished manuscript. Bozeman, MT: Montana State University.

Harrigan, J. J. (1984). *Politics and Policy in States and Communities, Instructor's Manual.* Boston, MA: Little, Brown and Co.

Henderson, A. (1981, 1987, 1988, 1991) *The Evidence Continues To Grow.* Washington, DC: National Committee for Citizens in Education, (70) 148-53 (October).

Henderson, A. (1988). "Parents Are a School's Best Friends," *Phi Delta Kappan.*

Henderson, A., Marburger, C., and Ooms, T. (1987). "Building a Family-School Relationship," *Principal,* (January).

Henderson, A., Marburger, C., and Ooms, T. (1986). *Beyond the Bake Sale.* Washington, DC: National Committee for Citizens in Education.

Herrick, S. and Epstein, J. (1990). *Implementing School and Family Partnerships in the Elementary Grades: Two Evaluations of Reading Activity Packets and School Newsletters.* (CDS Report No. 19.) Baltimore, MD: Johns Hopkins University Center for Research on the Effective Schooling for Disadvantaged Students.

Hodgkinson, H. (1992). *A Demographic Look at Tomorrow.* Washington, DC.: Institute for Educational Leadership.

Hodgkinson, H. (September 1991). "Reform vs. Reality." *Phi Delta Kappan.*

Hodgkinson, H. (1989). *The Same Client: The Demographics of Education and Service Delivery Systems.* Washington, DC: Institute for Educational Leadership.

Hoffer, T. B., and Coleman, J. S. (1990). "Changing Families and Communities: Implications for Schools," *Educational Leadership and Changing Contexts of Families, Communities, and Schools. Eighty-Ninth Yearbook of the National Society for the Study of Education, Part II.* B. Mitchell and L. L. Cunningham, eds. Chicago, IL: National Society for the Study of Education.

Johnson, V. R. (1993). *Parent/Family Centers: Dimensions of Functioning in 28 Schools in 14 States. Report No. 20* (September). Baltimore, MD: Center on Families, Communities, Schools and Children's Learning.

Kellaghan, T.; Sloane, K.; Alvarez, B.; and Bloom, B. S. (1993). *The Home Environment and School Learning.* San Francisco: Jossey-Bass.

Kids Count Data Book (1993). Washington, D.C.: Center for the Study of Social Policy.

Liontos, L. B. (1991). *Involving the Families of At-Risk Youth in the Educational Process. Trends and Issues Series, Number 5.* Eugene, OR: ERIC Clearinghouse on Educational Management, ED 328 946.

Liontos, L. B. (1990). *At-Risk Families and Schools, Becoming Partners.* Eugene, OR: ERIC Clearinghouse on Educational Management.

Margolis, H., and Tewel, K. (1988). "Resolving Conflict with Parents: A Guide for Administrators." *NASSP Bulletin.* (72)506, (March).

Marx, G. (1993). *Tips for Dealing with Pressure Groups.* Lecture and handout, Arlington, VA: American Association of School Administrators.

Moles, O. C., and D'Angelo, D. (1993). *Building School-Family Partnerships for Learning: Workshops for Urban Educators.* Washington, DC: U.S. Department of Education, OERI.

National Coalition of Partners in Education (no date). *Developing Family/School Partnerships: Guidelines for Schools and School Districts.*

National PTA (1987). "Parent Involvement: What Your PTA Can Do" in *Journal of Educational Public Relations.* (9)4.

National School Boards Association (November 1988). *First Teachers: Parental Involvement in the Public Schools.* Alexandria, VA.

National School Public Relations Association (no date). *Helping Parents Help Their Kids.* Arlington, VA.

"Parent Involvement: What Your PTA Can Do," *Journal of Educational Public Relations.* (8)4 Camp Hill, PA.

Public Education Awareness Committee (1990). *Family Involvement Campaign Overview.* Tallahassee, FL.

Red Carpet School: Family Involvement Campaign Overview. (No date). Tallahassee, FL: Florida Department of Education.

Rich, D. (1988). *MegaSkills — How Families Can Help Children Succeed in School and Beyond.* Boston, MA: Houghton Mifflin Co.

Smith, R. C., Lincoln, C., and Dodson, D. (1991). *Let's Do It Our Way: Working Together for Educational Excellence.* Chapel Hill, NC: MDC, Inc.

Swap, S. (1993). *Developing Home-School Partnerships: From Concepts to Practice.* New York, NY: Teachers College Press.

Swap, S. (1991). *Enhancing Parent Involvement in Schools.* New York, NY: Teachers College Press.

Swap, S. (1991). "Can Parent Involvement Lead to Increased Student Achievement in Urban Schools?" Paper presented at the Annual Meeting of the American Educational Research Association(ED 333 079).

Swap, S. (1990). *Parent Involvement and Success for All Children: What We Know Now.* Boston, MA: Institute for Responsive Education.

The Parent Institute (1993). "Provide Parent Education Classes in Parents' Workplace and Watch Involvement Grow," *What's Working in Parent Involvement* (February).

Tizard, J., Schofield, W., and Hewison, J. (1982). "Collaboration between Teachers and Parents in Assisting Children's Reading, *British Journal of Educational Psychology,* 52(1).

Vandegrift, J. and Green, A. (1992). "Rethinking Parent Involvement," *Educational Leadership*, (September).

Walberg, H., Bole, R., and Waxman, H. (1980). "School-Based Family Socialization and Reading Achievement in the Inner City," *Psychology in the Schools,* 17.

Weinberg, P. (1990). *Family Literacy and the School, How Teachers Can Help*. Syracuse, NY: New Readers Press.

Wikelund, K. (1990). *Schools and Communities Together: A Guide to Parent Involvement.* Portland, OR: Northwest Regional Educational Laboratory.

Williams, D., and Chavkin, N. (1985). *Guidelines and Strategies To Train Teachers for Parent Involvement.* Austin, TX: Southwestern Educational Development Laboratory.

RESOURCES

Many helpful resources are available to help develop or improve parent involvement programs. Some of the following organizations provide training and consulting services; all provide various types of printed materials.

Alliance for Parental Involvement in Education
P.O. Box 59
East Chatham, NY 12060-0059
(518) 392-6900

American Association of School Administrators
1801 N. Moore St.
Arlington, VA 22209-9988
(703) 875-0748

American Federation of Teachers
555 New Jersey Ave. NW
Washington, DC 20001
(202) 879-4400

ASPIRA Association Inc.
1112 16th St. NW, #340
Washington, DC 20036
(202) 835-3600

Center on Families, Communities, Schools, and Children's Learning
The Johns Hopkins University
3505 N. Charles St.
Baltimore, MD 21218
(410) 516-8800

Center for Law and Education
1875 Connecticut Ave. NW, Suite 510
Washington, DC 20009
(202) 462-7688

Child and Family Policy Center
100 Court Ave., Suite 312
Des Moines, IA 50309
(515) 280-9027

Children's Defense Fund
25 E St. NW
Washington, DC 20001
(202) 828-8787

Coalition of Essential Schools
Brown University
P.O. Box 1938
Providence, RI 02912
(401) 863-3384

Council of Chief State School Officers
One Massachusetts Ave. NW, Suite 700
Washington, DC 20001
(202) 408-5505

Council for American Private Education
1726 M St. NW, #1102
Washington, DC 20036
(202) 659-0016

Education Commission of the States
707 17th St., Suite 2700
Denver, CO 80204
(303) 299-3600

Family Resource Coalition
200 S. Michigan Ave., 16th floor
Chicago, IL 60604
(312) 341-0900

Hispanic Policy Development Project
250 Park Ave. South, Suite 500A
New York, NY 1003
(212) 529-9323

Home and School Institute
1500 Massachusetts Ave. NW
Washington, DC 20005
(202) 466-3633

Institute for Educational Leadership
1001 Connecticut Ave. NW, Suite 310
Washington, DC 20036
(202) 822-8405

Institute for Responsive Education
605 Commonwealth Ave.
Boston, MA 02215
(617) 353-3309

International Reading Association
800 Barksdale Rd., P.O. Box 8139
Newark, DE 19174-8139
(302) 731-1600

Mexican American Legal Defense and
Educational Fund
634 S. Spring St., 11th floor
Los Angeles, CA 90014
(213) 629-2512

National Association for the Education of
Young Children
1509 16th St. NW
Washington, DC 20036
(202) 232-8777

National Association of Elementary School
Principals
1615 Duke St.
Alexandria, VA 22314-3483
(703) 684-3345

National Association of Partners in
Education
209 Madison St., Suite 401
Alexandria, VA 22314
(703) 836-4880

National Association of School Psychologists
8455 Colesville Rd., Suite 1000
Silver Spring, MD 20910-3319
(301) 608-0500

National Association of Secondary School
Principals
1904 Association Dr.
Reston, VA 22091
(703) 860-0020

National Association of State Boards of
Education
1012 Cameron St.
Alexandria, VA 22314
(703) 684-4000

National Black Child Development Institute
1463 Rhode Island Ave. NW
Washington, DC 20005
(202) 387-1281

National Coalition for an Urban Children's
Agenda
c/o NASBE
1012 Cameron St.
Alexandria, VA 22314
(703) 684-4000

National Coalition of Title I/Chapter I
Parents
9th and D Sts. NE, Room 201
Washington, DC 20002
(202) 547-9286

National Community Education Association
3929 Old Lee Highway, Suite 91-A
Fairfax, VA 22030-2401
(703) 359-8973

National Council of La Raza
801 First St. NE, Suite 300
Washington, DC 20002-4205
(202) 289-1380

National Education Association
1201 16th St. NW
Washington, DC 20036
(202) 822-7015

National Parent Teacher Association
700 N. Rush St.
Chicago, IL 60611-2571
(312) 787-0977

National School Boards Association
1680 Duke St.
Alexandria, VA 22314
(703) 838-6722

National Urban League
500 E. 62nd St.
New York, NY 10021
(212) 310-9214

The Parent Institute
P.O. Box 7474
Fairfax Station, VA 22039
(703) 323-9170

Parents as Teachers National Center
University of Missouri - St. Louis
9374 Olive St.
St. Louis, MO 63132
(314) 432-4330

Parent Training and Information Centers
Technical Assistance to Parent Projects
95 Berkeley St., Suite 104
Boston, MA 02116
(617) 482-2915

School Improvement Council Assistance (SICA)
University of South Carolina
College of Education, Room 023
Columbia, SC 29208
(803) 777-7658

www.ingramcontent.com/pod-product-compliance
Lightning Source LLC
Chambersburg PA
CBHW061351300426
44116CB00011B/2082